Creative Learning & Living

The Human Element

Moira T. Carley, Ed.D.

Dear Roger,
Thank you for all the rides
& conversations and work
on our VMM committee
Cecily

Thomas More Institute Papers

Montreal 2005

Cover design by Typoscript
Cover painting by Robert Nagy

Thomas More Institute Papers, 2005
3405 Atwater Avenue, Montréal, Qc Canada H3H 1Y2

Note for Librarians: A cataloguing record for this book is available from Library and Archives Canada at www.collectionscanada.ca/amicus/index-e.html
ISBN 1-4120-5875-9

Printed in Victoria, BC, Canada. Printed on paper with minimum 30% recycled fibre. Trafford's print shop runs on "green energy" from solar, wind and other environmentally-friendly power sources.

TRAFFORD

Offices in Canada, USA, Ireland and UK
This book was published *on-demand* in cooperation with Trafford Publishing. On-demand publishing is a unique process and service of making a book available for retail sale to the public taking advantage of on-demand manufacturing and Internet marketing. On-demand publishing includes promotions, retail sales, manufacturing, order fulfilment, accounting and collecting royalties on behalf of the author.

Book sales for North America and international:
Trafford Publishing, 6E–2333 Government St.,
Victoria, BC v8t 4p4 CANADA
phone 250 383 6864 (toll-free 1 888 232 4444)
fax 250 383 6804; email to orders@trafford.com
Book sales in Europe:
Trafford Publishing (uk) Ltd., Enterprise House, Wistaston Road Business Centre,
Wistaston Road, Crewe, Cheshire cw2 7rp UNITED KINGDOM
phone 01270 251 396 (local rate 0845 230 9601)
facsimile 01270 254 983; orders.uk@trafford.com
Order online at:
trafford.com/05-0776

10 9 8 7 6 5 4 3 2 1

Acknowledgements

I thank all my students over the years who taught me how to teach, for the joy of it!

Students in the Creative Self course at Lonergan University College, Concordia from 1992-2003 deserve special thanks for their collaboration in this project of making accessible Bernard Lonergan's thought on human understanding.

I thank my family and friends who listened and read and cheered me on with love.

I thank the Lonergan scholars who helped me to interpret his thought and befriended me as I worked to make it accessible to educators. Robert Doran, Matthew Lamb, Frederick Lawrence, Sebastian Moore, Brian Cronin, Frederick Crowe, Joseph Flanagan, Timothy Lynch, Philippe Fluri, Tad Dunne.

I thank the Center for Studies of Religion and Society at the University of Victoria, British Columbia, for the fellowship and the space that allowed me to begin to write. The Concordia University Part time Faculty Association, CUPFA, have been most generous in their support over the years. The Thomas More Institute for Adult Education has provided constant and generous encouragement and support beginning with Anthony Joseph who guided my first reading of Insight in 1975 and continuing today with Charlotte Tansey, Judith Gray and all who have become the wind at my back as this project comes to completion.

I thank Robert Nagy for the art work on the cover, his friendship and his words: *I have made a sun in eclipse because the hazy horizon of the fiery ball teases us into wondering and imagining what reality must be like.*

I thank Israel Scheffler, Emeritus Professor at Harvard Graduate School of Education, to whom I dedicate this book, in remembrance of the day I heard him utter the words that every student should hear from a teacher at least once in a lifetime: *the world needs to hear what you have to say!*

Table of Contents

To view past works – whether of art or science or architecture, or music, or literature or mathematics, or history, or religion, or philosophy – as given and unique objects rather than as incarnations of process is to close off the traditions of effort from which they emerged.

It is to bring these traditions to a full stop…

Appreciating the underlying process does not, by any means, exhaust the possibilities of understanding. But the understanding it does provide is a ground of further creativity in thought and action.

Israel Scheffler, In Praise of Cognitive Emotions

Introduction

Most university students come to school with a hunting and gathering attitude that says *tell me what I need to know to get the piece of paper and get out of here.* They have already endured years in school passively receiving other people's knowledge without ever experiencing the transforming effect of their own intelligence at work or the excitement of understanding something for themselves. Artificial intelligence has made accessible to human fingertips mountains of information that can be transmitted to the grooves and chemicals of human brains. Yet, unless human intelligence grasps the presence (or absence) of intelligible patterns of meaning in the data, students remain mere receptacles of information.

The fact that computers can do so much for students – even write their papers supplies a new incentive to ask questions about the diminishing human element in the teaching-learning process. When thirty-two commerce students submitted identical papers taken from the internet, there was a flurry of excitement about plagiarism in the local press, but not much interest in the teaching strategy that could have allowed this to happen.

Can an ideal of education be re-imagined that includes a teaching strategy that encourages students to respond critically to data by using their own minds to follow through on questions? The human exchange between teacher and student – once thought essential to the teaching-learning process – has disappeared from the very structure of educational systems beyond the primary level. Where is the human element to be found in education today?

In his signature book, *Insight: A Study of Human Understanding,* the Canadian philosopher-theologian, Bernard Lonergan (1904-1984) claims that human learning flourishes best when students experience their own minds at work asking questions and finding answers for themselves.[1] As a long time student of Lonergan's work, I have mined his work on human understanding to uncover a model of teaching and learning that suggests a new educational ideal for our times.

About ten years ago, after completing a doctoral thesis at Harvard Graduate School of Education on *Bernard Lonergan: On Teaching*, I developed a university course I call *The Creative Self*, based on Lonergan's explanation of how humans usually come to knowledge of what is real or true or valuable. The course is structured on Lonergan's theory of how the human mind follows a spiraling process of heightening consciousness from being attentive to data, to intelligent questioning, to making reasonable judgments based on available evidence, to becoming a responsible maker of value decisions. Before students are introduced to Lonergan's thought as theory, they have experienced themselves being attentive, intelligent, reasonable and responsible learners. As they first experience and then reflect on their own learning process, students in the course discover that what they assumed to be abstract ideas about reality, truth and values are in fact rooted in the concrete living of ordinary lives — their own. The *habitus* of heightened human consciousness or awareness has transformed their way of being in the world. They have come to recognize themselves as free human beings, capable of asking questions and finding answers for themselves.

As students verify for themselves Lonergan's explanation (cognitional theory) of how their own minds work, they make connections between what they are learning and what they are living. This quote came from Danielle with a note attached: *This is just a small gift – I saw the connection between this vision and what we have been doing – chances are you've already read it.* I had not read it, but this small gift strengthened my desire to teach so that students would learn for themselves.

The erotic is a measure between the beginning of our sense of self and the chaos of our strongest feelings. It is an internal sense of satisfaction to which, once we have experienced it, we know we can aspire. For having experienced the fullness of this depth of feeling and recognizing its power, in honor and self-respect we can require no less of ourselves. To encourage excellence is to go beyond the encouraged mediocrity of our society, is to encourage excellence. But giving in to the fear of feeling and working to capacity is a luxury only the unintentional can afford, and the unintentional are those who do not wish to guide their own destinies.[2]

When the goal of teaching is the achievement of student-learning, class preparation changes from how to transmit already-out-there-knowledge to how to engage students to follow through on their own real questions. The teacher who intends learning will search for stories, interviews, film clips or reading material that suggest images that resonate with students' experience so they can unpack these images with their own questions. The teaching strategy changes radically from telling a captive audience what they need to know to actively engaging students in the rhythms of their own learning process. Success or failure in the classroom can be measured by the evidence of students' interest and willingness to follow through on their own questions, instead of how well they give back what they have been told.

Bernard Lonergan identified educators of his day as important agents of change in history when he challenged them to become creative collaborators within the educational system, not personalities who are *sunk into the existing situation…like cogs in a wheel with little grasp of possibilities, with a lack of daring.*[3] His words apply even more dramatically to today's system that needs to restore to the teaching-learning process the freedom and capacity of the human mind. During a casual conversation with some friends who are educators, they asked what it was exactly I was writing about: *It's about allowing students to use their own minds to learn. It's about freeing their imagination and intelligence so they can learn on their own.* One woman with many years' experience in the schools replied without a blink: *But the system certainly wouldn't allow that!*

In a series of lectures given to educators in 1959, Lonergan speaks as a teacher who has often wondered just what he was contributing to students' learning. *What I want to communicate…The great task that is* demanded if we are to make (life) livable again is the re-creation of the liberty of the subject, the recognition of the freedom of consciousness.[4] He reflects critically on the function of education within specific cultural, social and religious horizons. He challenges educators to ask themselves: What is the good of education for my students? How does the understanding of human good change in history? In culture? How does education contribute to human living? What is this new learning in our times?

Later, in an essay written in 1977, *Natural Right and Historical Mindedness,* Lonergan comments on the goal of education within the context of the evolving historical human community. The natural right of all human beings is the freedom to learn and to evolve in history. Historicity, he says, is most conspicuous in the educational community because it is there that developing human beings create the only edition of themselves that the world will come to know. The human choice to learn and live creatively is a free response to the *tidal movement that begins before consciousness, unfolds through sensitivity, intelligence, rational reflection, responsible deliberation, only to find its rest beyond all these...an ongoing process of self-transcendence.*[5]

Before leaving the question of what Lonergan's thought on human learning contributes to education today, I want to address the issue of his own religious faith which, for those who do not share his adherence to the Christian tradition, may diminish the value of what he has to say about teaching and learning.

As I understand it, Lonergan's explanation of the human capacity to come to knowledge emerges from his belief, shared with Thomas Aquinas, that human minds have the capacity to share in the wisdom of that which is called "God."...*the reason why we know is within us...the intellectual light which we have within us is nothing else than a certain participated likeness of the uncreated light.*[6] In other words, along with the capacity for human inquiry comes a mandate to question without restriction. Knowledge is not to be found in a library or in the teachings of authorities of the past but in the activity of the human mind asking questions within *the pulsing flow of life.* No one knew better than he did the multitude of ways that human persons are drawn to understand what is true or real or valuable.

Religious faith, for Lonergan, is born of one's awareness of being loved by God. Knowledge of this awareness cannot be exhaustively articulated from one generation to the next. Religious faith ushers us into a *friendly universe* where each generations' questions soar toward the mystery. Religious faith, for Lonergan, does not limit the human mind's capacity to come to knowledge, but provides a flourishing environment of love in which questions are free to arise. The very question that stretches the human spirit toward the *region for the divine*, becomes for Lonergan, *a shrine for ultimate holiness.*[7] It is this horizon of love and awe that he offers to all who would learn from him.

This book is written out of my own desire to make accessible to readers the freedom and capacity of their own minds to learn what is real or true or valuable. It is my own attempt to contribute the human element to the educational system of our time by engaging students in their own learning process. It is written with the conviction that human intelligence flourishes best when teachers and students creatively collaborate in the teaching-learning process.

Chapter One: *What do we do when we teach?* tells the story of my own efforts to follow through on this question and to understand *why* certain teaching methods contribute (or not!) to student learning. A teaching strategy developed from my experience, understanding and critical reflection on Lonergan's cognitional theory is explained. Chapter Two: *Creativity and Insight,* illustrates how the engine of the question seeks an intelligible pattern in the data (image) and achieves insight or understanding. Chapter Three: *Imagination,* illustrates how images help or hinder students' ability to learn for themselves. The creative collaboration of intelligence and imagination is key to understanding Lonergan's thought on human learning. Chapter Four: *Creativity and Consciousness,* makes the connection between creativity and consciousness and demonstrates how heightened human consciousness evolves as the question spirals from understanding towards critical reflection and eventually judgment of knowledge. The *why* of teaching strategy is explored against the background of the imperatives: be attentive, be intelligent, be reasonable, be responsible.

Chapter Five: *Creativity and Values,* introduces moral consciousness as the ultimate goal of the educational process, when creative learning becomes embedded in one's conscious living. Through deliberation, evaluation and decision, the learner comes to heightened awareness of the self. Chapter Six: *Creativity and Self-transcendence,* follows the lead of those students who have asked: *where do we go from here?* An imaginary dialogue with Lonergan, the teacher, has him listening to their questions and drawing them into the presence of Mystery experienced as Love and Awe.

Because so many people find Lonergan's writing dense and difficult — it is a rigorous read — I have deliberately avoided the specialized language used by Lonergan scholars. His theory of human understanding can make an important and much needed contribution to the educational system of our times because it assumes the presence of the human element on both sides of the desk. I want to make his thought accessible to people who value the human exchange in education but will not read his work *straight.*

The educational ideal that underpins this book is the discovery of oneself as a consciously free and intelligent person, willing and able to engage in creative learning and living in our times. In the writing it has become a story of my own practice in the classroom attempting to contribute the human element to education. It has also become the story of students yielding to my desire to engage them in their own learning and suggesting that I *write it down!*

The Lord God has given me
the tongue of a teacher,
that I may know how to sustain the weary with a word.
Morning by morning he wakens –
wakens my ear
to listen as those who are taught.

(Isaiah 50:4)

1. What do we do when we teach?

the question arises...

Many years ago, during my first year teaching at the university, after what I thought was a fairly engaging lecture, and hoping for some response from the sixty students in front of me, I asked them: *What do you think?* An answer I didn't expect came from a long-legged young man sitting in the front row. Continuing to look down at his notebook, he muttered loud enough for me to hear, *Who the hell cares?*

That was when I came to understand that students who sit in class filling their notebooks with *my* knowledge soon lose interest in learning for themselves. They learn to survive the drudgery of school by slipping into a state of robotic passivity.

I have since come to realize that most university students commonly spend four years in school working hard for a diploma without ever experiencing the excitement of their own minds at work learning something new. That they can bring their own active intelligence to the learning process is beyond what they can imagine. "Unbelievable!" they say when they are asked to express their own thoughts and questions in their own words.

The larger tragedy, as I see it, is that when the spontaneous human desire to question and to understand and to create meaning is not actively engaged in the teaching/learning process, humanity is diminished. The zone of imagination shrinks. Boredom and despair set in. The young inner life ripe for expansion shrivels up for lack of hope. As students learn to play the game of accumulating other people's knowledge, the curiosity and wonder that five-year-olds bring to school, is educated out of them. When I asked my then twenty-year-old nephew, Michael John, once a child totally turned on by curiosity about the world, what he had learned in his first year of university, he said: *I learned how to pass exams.*

Though I had been teaching religion to children, adolescents and adults for almost twenty years, and had acquired some confidence as a teacher, when I joined the Faculty of Education at McGill University in Montreal, I hadn't yet figured out *why* some things worked for me in the classroom and others did not. Faced with the task of teaching student teachers how to teach, I had no theory to explain the *why* of teaching practice. I suddenly had an urgent question to answer: What do we *do* when we teach? And *why*?

the journey...

Instinctively, I knew that a recipe for teaching – as in five easy steps – would not help students to function in their teaching /learning situation. A single cookie-cutter strategy would not do because in any exchange with human beings there are no certainties. What was needed was a strategy that would embody the teacher's active intelligence in pursuit of a purpose (student learning) and also one that was resilient enough to free student teachers to ask and follow through on their own questions about teaching when they found themselves actually working with students of their own.

In May, 1975, I attended a lecture by Bernard Lonergan at the Thomas More Institute for Adult Learning in Montreal. I listened as he spoke about *Healing and Creating in History,* understanding little and feeling confused and disappointed at the end of the evening as I watched him walk slowly out of the large hall. I stood behind a pillar to get a better look. As he passed, our eyes met, he nodded, and I found myself reaching out to shake his hand and saying: *Thank you, Father Lonergan. Some of my best teachers have been inspired by your work.* His mouth dropped open in apparent surprise, and then the blue eyes sparkled as he said: *Thank you, my dear, I needed to hear something like that tonight.*

I am not sure why I feel compelled to share this story with every group of students that I now introduce to Lonergan's thought. Perhaps I want them to understand something of the fragility of the man who wrote...*even with talent, knowledge makes a slow, if not a bloody entrance. To learn thoroughly...calls for relentless perseverance. To strike out on a new line and become more than a weekend celebrity calls for years in which one's living is more or less constantly absorbed in the effort to understand.*[1] Perhaps they will agree with me that the questions that move us to make the effort to learn something new are usually stirred into life by another human being. Perhaps they too will marvel at the mysterious effect we have on one another as we struggle to find meaning as we create a life for ourselves.

The year after my brief meeting with Lonergan, I joined a group of adult learners at the Thomas More Institute to read the first thirteen chapters of his book, *Insight: A Study of Human Understanding.* In the mysterious ongoing experience of living and learning, it seems that I was beginning the journey that would lead me thirteen years later to Harvard Graduate School of Education and to the question that would inform my doctoral dissertation: *if we accept Lonergan's answer to the question of what we do when we come to know, what would we do when we teach?*

Robert Doran has said that Lonergan's own struggle to achieve a method of doing and teaching theology came out of his need to reconcile the ideal of a system with the reality of history within a framework for collaborative creativity.[2]

I wonder now if my own search for a theoretical basis for teaching came to me out of a similar need. At the time, the educational system was becoming heavy on information processing and light on the search for understanding. Daily, I met students who wanted to be told what they needed to know so that they could record it in their notebooks and give it back on exams and get the credentials they needed to become teachers. For them, to *learn* meant to passively receive other people's knowledge. The notion that learning required their own engaged intelligence was simply beyond them.

When Lonergan's lecture on *Healing and Creating in History* appeared in print and I had read it several times, I understood better what he had been saying when I heard him speak. Soon, these words began ringing in my ears: *When survival requires a system that does not exist, then the need for creating it is manifest.*[3] I wondered how to create an educational system that would engage students in their own learning.

Meanwhile, at the Thomas More Institute, we continued to help one another plow through Lonergan's book *Insight*. He said that his intention was to provide readers with a pedagogical exercise that would illustrate their own dynamic intelligence at work. But in the first five chapters, he cites so many different kinds of insight, assuming that his readers have his facility with the language and theory of mathematics, physics, philosophy, and science. Many willing learners feel inadequate (stupid, even) lose interest and give up trying to understand even before reaching the end of chapter five. It seemed that Lonergan expected too much of the general reader and I knew my students would not be willing to read him "straight."

Still, I suspected that he had something to teach the world about human understanding and my own experience of *needing to know* kept curiosity on the move as I struggled to make my own what he was saying about the act of insight. My question about what we *do* when we teach was kept alive in the friendly home provided by my friends at the Thomas More Institute.

After a lot more study and generous help from a series of guides, I finally grasped what I consider to be the core genius of Lonergan's book, *Insight. Our faculty of understanding abstracts the intelligible forms from images...also it grasps the forms in images, for it has no capacity whatever for understanding...except by turning to images.*[4]

Since insight or understanding is an act of human intelligence grasping the intelligible pattern in the image, then what we *do* when we teach is to supply helpful images and questions to engage students in their own learning. Teachers contribute to learning when they clear the way for students to understand for themselves. Students learn when they ask and follow through on their own questions. I had identified the *why* that informed the strategy I used when students actually learned what I was hoping to teach. Lonergan's theory of what we do when we come to know helped me to understand why it had worked in the classroom.

Lonergan on teaching...

In chapter six of *Insight*, "Common Sense and its Subject" Lonergan makes this rare explicit reference to what teachers contribute to students' learning.

If we really would master the answers, we somehow have to find them out ourselves. Such learning is not without teaching. For teaching is the communication of insight. It throws out the clues, the pointed hints that lead to insight. It cajoles attention to drive away the distracting images that stand in insight's way. It puts the further questions that reveal the need of further insights to modify and complement the acquired store. It has grasped the strategy of developing intelligence, and so begins from the simple to advance to the more complex...to make the achievement of each successive generation the starting point of the next.[5]

Robert Doran says that Lonergan told him that the two chapters on Common Sense were written first when he began the work of *Insight* and that they *contained what he most wanted to say, i.e. the role of human intelligence in history and society and the relation of intelligence to social and cultural progress and decline.*[6]

By including his thought on what teachers do within the chapters on Common Sense, it seems that Lonergan wanted his readers to understand that what we *do* when we teach is *done* within the realm of common sense meaning. When he says that *teaching is the communication of insight* he is also calling attention to the need for the teacher to engage the intelligence of the learner. Insight is something achieved by someone with a question. Each person must do it for oneself. Teaching is not talking or telling students what they need to know, it is communicating with another *incarnate intelligence.*

Lonergan makes a distinction between learners who function in the realm of scientific intelligence and are concerned with theory (how things relate to one another) and learners who function in the realm of common sense intelligence and are concerned with understanding concrete experience (how things relate to oneself). This distinction is often overlooked by teachers even by those teaching Lonergan's thought. A teaching strategy that aims to engage the learner in his or her own learning would expect that teachers:

- use language that students understand.
- not tell students everything they need to know about a subject.
- ask questions that can lead to insights – open the way for students to achieve further insights – their own.
- communicate with students where they are now.

Instead of aiming to transmit universally valid knowledge, or using technical language, teachers who intend to engage students' intelligence will communicate in the realm of common sense meaning because, says Lonergan, common sense intelligence:

- has no technical language;
- does not aspire to universally valid knowledge (theory) or laws;
- operates from an accumulation of incomplete insights and open questions;
- communicates with a particular person about a concrete situation.[7]

An example: While supervising a student-teacher who was telling the biblical story of King David to a group of eighth-grade boys, I heard a student ask this question: *If David was such a good friend of God's why did he get into so many fights and wars?* To which the practicing teacher replied: *That's not part of the story!* I was disappointed that he dismissed what I assumed to be a genuine question and a potent learning opportunity. When I asked him about it later he explained: *Oh, David, yes he's always trying to get me off track.* The questioner's name was David too! Here was a 20th century eighth-grade David reaching for understanding but cut off before he could reach his goal.

Israel Scheffler, philosopher of education, Emeritus professor at Harvard, and my own former teacher, describes teaching as that intentional activity *aimed at the achievement of learning and practiced in such a manner as to respect the student's intellectual integrity and capacity for independent judgment.*[8]

All this to say that Lonergan's answer to the question of what teachers do when we teach would be: *to find a way for students to learn for themselves by following through on their own questions.* Too often insecurity or the need for control makes teachers treat questions as unwelcome interruptions that have nothing to do with what we want students to learn.

Still, it is naïve to think there will be no deliberate deflections! My own first conscious memory of the fun of learning comes from a time when we used to deflect a certain new teacher from the planned curriculum by asking an endless list of questions. We thought we were fooling her, but now I realize she knew exactly what she was doing when she allowed our questions to prevail. By turning us on to the excitement of our own minds at work she unleashed our floundering adolescence into a friendly universe and gave us freedom to learn how to learn for ourselves. The best and most available resource for the teacher who wants to have students learn is the latent curiosity of the human spirit waiting to be stirred into life by a question. Says Lonergan:

Deep within us all, emergent when the noise of other appetites is stilled, there is a drive to know, to understand, to see why, to discover the reason, to find the cause, to explain. Just what is wanted has many names. In what precisely it consists is a matter of dispute. But the fact of inquiry is beyond all doubt.[9]

a teaching strategy...

The teaching-learning strategy that I have developed from my study of Lonergan's work and validated in my own classroom is based on these three assumptions:

- Students come to school with the natural desire and capacity to understand for themselves – *they have questions.*
- Teachers engage students in their own learning – *they have intelligence.*
- Students are expected to express what they have learned in some creative form – *they have understood.*

In Lonergan's scheme, the teacher is an artist creating out of the materials at hand with...*all the delicacy and subtlety, all the rapidity and effectiveness, with which one incarnate intelligence can communicate its grasp to another by grasping what the other has yet to grasp and what act or sound or sign would make him grasp it.*[10]

My own class preparation is often messy and flawed, but real as life itself as I search for the right *act or sound or sign* to draw students into their own learning. I work out of a framework for teaching/learning constructed of: *images – questions – insights – responses.*

how images...lead to questions

Like a detective looking for the clue that will crack the case, I track down images that can engage students in their own questions. I also jot down questions that I hope will keep other distracting images away. Video clips from the evening news, excerpts from a film, a poem, an interview, a short story or novel, an invited guest, create a shared experience that leaves behind an image for us to unpack with questions. An interesting character in a short story is usually a good image to explore with questions. When students respond by asking their own questions, I feel grateful. When they don't get it, I might prod with my own questions and search and try again for another image to catch their interest. I have learned to listen for the nuanced expressions of what seems "real" for them. Since every class session has become a learning experience for me as well, I record and critically evaluate the level of involvement (or not) and ask myself: *What happened? Why? What needs to be done next?*

Like antenna crackling with electricity connecting the experience of our inner and outer worlds, the image offers patterns or clues to the questions that lead to insight. Images provide a safe place to roam while questions come to the surface of consciousness. Images are key to awakening students' questions about the meaning of experience: *what's going on here? why?* A teacher who happens upon the right image – one that resonates with students' experience – will stand back in awe as their energy takes over the learning process.

An example: when Socrates wanted Meno's slave to understand the geometry of double squares, he used a diagram and he asked questions. He wanted the boy to both know for himself and to give an account of what he understood. It would have been easier to tell him what he needed to know, but Socrates, the archetypal teacher, understood that telling isn't teaching and because images hold the clue to finding out the answer for ourselves – real learning.

Another example: An image of a man in prison writing a letter to his wife describing how he wrote a letter to the authorities hoping to secure his release. The students are given an excerpt from the letter and discuss what happened to him as he reflected critically on his experience. The man said at the time of writing, he thought the letter was simply an act of *honorable cleverness*. Later, when he reflected on what he had written, he realized: *I overlooked the fact that truth lies not only in what is said, but also in who says it, and to whom, why, how and under what circumstances it is expressed.* The man was Vaclav Havel, soon to become President of the Czech Republic. The letter to his wife, Olga, had been written while in prison as a political dissident in 1982.[11] A student's response to the reading explains how the image started a stream of questions for her:

I have a friend who always says that growing up means taking responsibility for your actions. In the past, I've shrugged off this statement saying, "well, of course, you can't deny what you've done." After reading this article, my view of taking responsibility has changed drastically. It's not just admitting to your actions, and it's not even dealing with the consequences of those actions. It's accepting those actions as apart of yourself, and taking a serious look at that aspect of yourself. In doing so, a negative experience has a positive outcome in that it paves the way to self-realization...It is our responsibility to constantly redefine ourselves – identity is not a 'what' which is set in stone waiting to be discovered; rather, I now see it as a 'how.' How do you choose to approach life? By leaving identity open to change, we leave ourselves open to new experiences which in turn may lead us to new relationships, new discoveries, new levels of consciousness. (Sarah Etezadi-Amoli)[12]

questions...lead to insights

One year, a friend who is a sculptor brought his sculpture of St. Francis and his sketch book to my class. He sat in the back of the room as I asked students to walk around the statue and quietly experience the presence of the statue. Some responded hesitantly with their own impressions of wonder, tranquillity, awe, sadness. The artist told me later that aspects of his work of which he was unaware had been expressed by the students. He had a block of oak and a question: *could I make Francis come out of this?* When he put his sketch book on the table so they could see for themselves the evolving process of the work there was an electrifying response. We both backed off in amazement as we watched these university students suddenly become as uninhibited as kindergarten children. They pummeled him with questions: *Why are Francis' eyes closed? Why is he embracing a skeleton? What happened to the bird in his hands?* (there in the beginning sketches). *What was going on in you as you created this? Is it about death?*

When later students were asked to read what Lonergan had written about self appropriation and insight, how insight is achieved by grasping the intelligible pattern in an image as the learner moves from experience to question to understanding, the experience of the sculpture provided a vivid image to unpack. Reading Lonergan's words helped them to understand their own experience: insight or understanding is generated by a mind on the move asking questions of experience – more questions and new insights follow – until what is understood is given form, articulated in a word, a concept, a gesture, a sculpture, a life.

The work of learning begins when desire or curiosity stirs and takes form in a question. Teachers contribute to students' learning by facilitating their interest and encouraging them to follow through on their own questions. It seems obvious, but it is not. Students need to learn how to learn. Most of them are unaware that by asking their own questions, ones for which *they* really need answers, they engage in their own learning process. After reading an essay on how insight is achieved (an earlier version of the next chapter) one student wrote this:

After reading the paper, I feel messed up! I realized, in closely examining my previous belief, that I considered a person to be intelligent if they knew the answer, and to 'not know' the answer was to be unintelligent. Now I understand that to be intelligent is to actively 'not' have the answer, to be seeking an answer. Not having the answer is necessary to increased understanding...what I should be striving for and not avoiding at all costs. At some point I had decided that anything that would put me in a position of not knowing, or of not knowing completely, I veered away from...a gradual process of closing off experience...I stopped asking questions. What I did, effectively, was hurt myself deeply. (Christine Harkness)

Observing how insights happen in other people helps us to recognize a similar process happening in ourselves. A video clip of a cartoon-like Einstein chasing a beam of light and asking: *If I caught a beam of light, what would I have?* illustrates how he pursued his own questions. Einstein's *thought experiments* always began with his own questions about the world. He didn't accept, for instance, (what he was taught in school) that the world was held together by something called *ether*. This concept – what someone else understood – didn't satisfy his curiosity. Einstein was a young man in search of answers for himself.

The distinction between insight and concept is crucial to Lonergan's understanding of what we do when we come to know. My own approach to teaching has been radically transformed by what I learned from him about the role of concepts in the learning process. If knowledge is the result of the dynamic act of intelligence, then knowledge cannot be handed on as a collection of concepts stored in the memory bank. So teachers who give *concepts* to their students without giving breathing room to the questions that resulted in the concepts, do not contribute to students' learning but to the contents of a memory bank. For Lonergan, knowledge is a cumulative process of human consciousness moving from experience to understanding to judgment. Concepts are expressions or formulations of what has been understood – already achieved insights. Concepts are like the period on a sentence – the end point of active learning. They contribute to judgments of what is true or real or valuable but they come at the end of the process. Insights, says Lonergan are incomplete – *a dime a dozen* – not yet the desired knowledge behind the question.

Insights, unlike concepts, keep learning on the move, open to more questions, more insights, more light on the issue. Concepts are like definitions, they mean just what they say and no more. They tend to close down inquiry because they are expressed in fixed terms – *this is how it is.* Teachers who teach only concepts to students without exploring as well the questions that led to the expression of knowledge – even Einstein's knowledge – begin at the wrong end of the learning process.

insights lead to creativity ...

One year, at the end of the Creative Self course, students were asked to write a letter to a friend sharing what they had learned about their own learning process from Lonergan's explanation of what we do when we come to know. This excerpt from one of the response papers says it well:

Imagine a system that provides a framework to guide students into their own discovery of the problem solving tools you need to learn...Now this is what is really cool. The course was set up to verify this idea. We went through the experience that created the tension of inquiry.... The course material raised problems that created the desire to know. We were all going nuts trying to figure out what was going on and then...we heard an interpretation of Lonergan's (cognitional) theory. Wham! It all fell into place. So this is THE key to learning and we were our own proof. (Ray Taylor)

An important part of Lonergan's theory is the learner's need to express in his or her own words what has been understood. What we have come to understand tentatively can reach new clarity as we express it to another. Expression is absolutely essential to the learning process. Or so I like to believe.

Toward the end of his 1959 lectures to educators Lonergan says that since mathematics, natural science, philosophy and psychology *are not the same as life,* art as the mirror of *concrete living in its concrete potentialities* connects learning with living. He aligns himself with the ancient philosophers who believed the goal of education to be learning how to live the good life.[13] Reading and re-reading this lecture, and listening to his spoken words on the compact disc recording now available, I think I get the point: it is the inevitability of form in human discourse that leads to the creative expression of what has been understood.

Art is the objectification of the experiential pattern of lived experience.[14] The spontaneous dynamism of intelligence on the move, becomes transparent to the other when expressed. Lonergan says that educators *concerned with the subject coming to be himself,* should accept the *fundamental fact that it is on the artistic symbolic level that we live.*[15]

Teachers who expect students to respond by expressing their own understanding, are creating a flourishing framework for freedom of consciousness and re-creation of imagination. When the fear of *not knowing* is replaced by re-imagining oneself as a learner on the way to understanding, new horizons of creativity are accessible to the learner. Artistic consciousness in the learning process replaces the philosophical presupposition of utilitarianism or the need to prove or convince or persuade the other.

One year my course included, for me, a daunting number of football players. I wondered how they would answer the response paper asking them how Lonergan's explanation of the levels of consciousness had helped them understand their own learning experience. As well as contributing to my limited football vocabulary, one of my students gave me a description of intelligence at work that came to him as he was puzzling over the essay question and watching a football game on TV (at the same time!)

...within five minutes of watching the game the running back for one team made a spectacular play breaking the tackles of numerous defenders to gallop 25 yards into the end zone. The announcer cried out with great enthusiasm: 'What a creative play by the running back!' and that is where it clicked. I asked myself these questions: what about this play was creative? Does something as simple as a 10-second football play have a deeper meaning? As fans and spectators we only see the physical actions of the player, but beneath these actions there is a whole layer of in-depth thought and creativity to make this spectacular action a reality. There is a common football saying that says "run to daylight." The metaphor means that to a running back everything that is a dangerous area is dark and shaded because there is normally a defender in that position, but his windows of opportunity normally appear where he can see a crack of daylight shining through the darkness, a weakness in the defense, an area of safety where he

can run. He must be very attentive and alert to watch and scan and ask himself when and where this opening will appear and how he will make the passage through. The imagination kicks in and gives him the clue and in this case he did a nifty little spin to get out of the grasp of the defender, and successfully hit his daylight hole, and marched into the end zone for the touchdown. Jeffrey said he was surprised to see that I had written the word *brilliant* on his paper.

Finally...

I imagine an extra thickness to the spine developing in students who have learned to think for themselves. They now stand with more confidence and agility in the learning process that is concrete living. The *habitus* of learning continues to unfold in their particular and concrete lives.

I have stomped my foot in despair when students dutifully copy what I've just said into their notebooks with no apparent interest in searching out answers for themselves. I have also stood back in admiration and awe when students let me know they are on a roll, asking genuine questions and savoring the dynamism of their own intelligence at work searching for answers. When they have come to understand more than I intended to teach and still want to know more, I still ask: *What did I do that was right? Can I make it happen again?*

The answer to the question of what we *do* when we teach gleaned from Lonergan's thought on what we do when we come to know requires an ongoing radical re-imagining of how teachers contribute to learning. I know now that the questions that beat at the wall of consciousness will never end. When the objective of teaching becomes the achievement of student learning, teachers create more work for ourselves before, during and after the time spent in the classroom. I agree with this remark from one of my colleagues: *Your method of teaching is so labor intensive!* And I know that the personal cost is more than time and effort. A teacher who wants simply to have students learn has given up control of the teaching/learning process. To replace the currently efficient *listen as I tell you what you need to know* teaching strategy with Lonergan's *one incarnate intelligence communicating with another incarnate intelligence,* is to share the empowerment that personal knowledge confers. Teachers who acknowledge their students' desire and capacity to learn for themselves will provide them with the tools to learn how to learn. They will also usher them into a friendly universe and beyond.

*Not only are men born with a native drive to inquire
and understand;*

*they are born into a community that possesses a common
fund of tested answers,*

*and from that fund each may draw his variable share,
measured by his capacity, his interests and his energy.*

*Not only does the self-correcting process of learning
unfold within the private consciousness of the individual;*

for by speech, and still more by example,

*there is effected a sustained communication that at once
disseminates and tests and improves every advance,*

*to make the achievement of each successive generation
the starting point of the next.*

Bernard Lonergan, Insight

2. Creativity and Insight –
we can all do it

The creative task, says Lonergan, *is a matter of insight, not of one insight but of many, not of isolated insights but of insights that coalesce, that complement and correct one another*…it is *nothing mysterious*.[1] In *Insight*, he tells us that we all have the capacity to achieve insight by asking real questions of life experience and following through on the desire to know as it spirals from one level of consciousness to the next.

Lonergan does not tell us *how* to achieve an insight. He does not offer a recipe to guide us through the learning process to a finished product. Instead, he guides the reader through a process of self awareness of how the human mind operates as it searches for understanding. In other words, if we pay attention to what we are doing when we risk asking questions of experience, questions as simple as: *What's going on? why?* we clear the way for understanding something for ourselves. His wants the reader to recognize the *banal* experience of insight as something he or she does all the time. He provides a dramatic instance of a particular insight that has become legendary – Archimedes running naked through the streets of Syracuse – and identifies in the story, the five psychological elements that make up the activity of the insight:

- It comes as a release to the tension of inquiry.
- It arrives suddenly and unexpectedly.
- It arises from inner conditions.
- It pivots between the concrete and the abstract.
- It is absorbed into the habitual texture of one's mind.[2]

another dramatic instance…

Following Lonergan's advice, one morning while making

coffee, I asked myself what I was doing when I heard a bell ringing and experienced the inner tension of a *why* question and finished up with some knowledge that I could claim as my own. Because, in the days before this experience, I had been reading *Insight* and puzzling over the five elements, I also came to identify the process of my own mind moving toward understanding and eventually knowledge.

I first became conscious of the fact that I had just understood something new. And then I had an insight into how I had actually had an insight.

I am standing in the kitchen and I hear a bell ringing from a distance, not in the kitchen. I feel myself wondering: Why? What is that? Imagination and memory kick in to help me answer the question. An image comes to the surface. A few days before, as I arrived home, I had heard a loud bell ringing and I saw the police inspecting a neighbor's house (they were away for the winter). Obviously, the alarm system had been activated. Now, my imagination holds the image of my neighbor's front door while I wonder if there is a connection between the sound I hear now and the sound I heard two days before: a pattern is forming helping me to concentrate on the image. I search the image with my questions: Is the alarm system making the noise? Why aren't the police there yet? Why is the bell ringing? I walk to the front door tense with inquiry. I see no evidence of police activity. As I turn back to the kitchen, another image comes in a flash – my alarm clock sounds like that – the pattern in my imagination has changed! It dawns on me that I had risen before the clock went off. Now I have come to understand something I didn't know before. I also understood the process of my own mind at work seeking understanding. The sound of a bell prompted the questions that became an engine moving me from an experience of mere sensation to an experience of intelligence grasping the meaning of what was going on. I had achieved an insight and I also understood for myself what Lonergan meant. I got it! I sat down at the table to enjoy my coffee and the new day.

Eureka! How it happens...

Archimedes' eureka experience provides the reader with a friendly space to ask questions about their own experience.

Hiero, new ruler of Syracuse, had provided craftsmen with an exact amount of gold by weight to make him a new crown. A rumour moved about Syracuse suggesting that some of the gold had been stolen and the weight made up with mere silver. How to be sure? Hiero asked Archimedes to figure it out. It was already known that silver has more volume than gold for the same weight, so an adulterated crown would be larger than one of pure gold. But the crown was so irregularly shaped that there was no way to compare it by volume with the same weight of gold. Worrying over this, Archimedes went off to the public baths. As he slipped into the bath water, he noticed that the deeper he settled, the more the water overflowed. His body was displacing the water. From this experience a surprise insight came: the volume of the crown could be measured by immersing it in water and observing the overflow. Archimedes had an answer to his question. The story has it that he ran naked through the streets of Syracuse shouting "Eureka!" which means in Greek "I've got it!"

The story gives us a classic image of insight achieved. It becomes for the reader a great working model of someone tuned into life experience, habitually wondering, and open to all possible answers.

Archimedes acts out for us the five elements in every act of insight.

- Here is a man tuned into life and asking real questions of experience, a man caught up in the *tension of inquiry.*
- Here is a man settling into the baths at Syracuse and *suddenly, unexpectedly grasping something new;*
- Here is intelligence-in-act showing us that *inner conditions were functioning.*
- Here is a man *moving from the concrete* – the gold in the crown and the sensation of water spilling over – *to abstract theory:* the laws of displacement and specific gravity.
- Here is a man *transformed* by what he has understood.

(1) Insight comes as a release to the tension of inquiry

A question is felt as tension before it is formulated in words. Desire – the primal energy of the human spirit – propels this feeling to search for meaning. Lonergan explains: *But the point I would make does not lie in this outburst of delight but in the antecedent desire and effort that it betrays...what better symbol could one find for this obscure, exigent, imperious drive, than a man, naked, running, excitedly crying, "I've got it?"*[3]

Archimedes did not go to the baths to discover the content of the gold crown. Presumably he went to bathe! At work, nonetheless, was the *antecedent desire* to understand, to find answers to the questions that worried him: Was the crown pure gold or not? How can I measure the content of the crown?

Questions that flow from *antecedent desire* seem to take on a life of their own as we follow their direction toward understanding. Before insights can arise in consciousness, the spontaneous dynamic pulse of life energy must be set free to unfold from awareness of experience to intelligent questions to the grasp of the intelligible pattern in the data.

Another experience helped me understand how crucial to the teaching-learning process is the *antecedent desire* of the learner. When I was working on my thesis, after a full day of writing, weary of the struggle to find words to express my own understanding of insight, I decided to go shopping for groceries. While dreamily pushing my cart along the aisle, I heard a child's voice calling out: *What's that?* Looking up, I saw a little boy in a grocery cart, turning around to his mother while his arm pointed to the live lobster aquarium. I heard the mother answer: *It's a lobster!* Then, as if he knew that I had been puzzling over the question of how we learn, the child shouted the question that philosophers love and parents dread: *Why?* His mother answered patiently, *because that's its name*, and pushed the grocery cart and the boy over to the cheese display.

I stood there wondering what was going on within the child. The image of a small boy with questions became a new focus for my own desire to understand what *antecedent desire* contributes to learning. He had been given the word *lobster* but that hadn't satisfied his desire or need or whatever was catapulting him from his space in the world to that of his mother's, so he asked *why??* And I asked myself, *what does he really want?*

The imperative force of his question made it clear that this was an expression of a real need: a passionate desire to understand. He wanted to *stand-under* the particular sense experience of the lobster. The word *lobster* had not satisfied his desire. Was this the clue? Was this what I was looking for? Could the desire to find an answer to a question be an essential condition of learning?

It was, in fact, the felt energy of the child's question that helped me to grasp the connection between *antecedent desire* and what Lonergan meant by insight beginning with the tension of inquiry. I also understood how easily dynamic human inquiry can be shot down in mid-flight. Lonergan claims that *what?* and *why?* are natural questions which come spontaneously from the primordial human desire to know the meaning of experience. *That drive, that desire to understand constitutes the primordial 'why?' Name it what you please, alertness of mind, intellectual curiosity, the spirit of inquiry, active intelligence, the drive to know.*[4]

Antecedent desire draws attention to the world of sense experience (the water overflowing in the baths of Syracuse, the king's crown, the moon following me home, or the lobster in a tank) and propels the movement of the human spirit toward questions for understanding. The tension of inquiry collapses when intelligible answers arise on the surface of consciousness. But words and concepts alone do not satisfy the primal desire expressed by *what? why?* What we really want is not a word only or another's understanding to repeat parrot-like, but when we ask a real question we want to *understand for ourselves.*

(2) Insight arrives suddenly and unexpectedly

Archimedes was obviously open to the surprise of discovery. His imagination was not limited by what he already knew. He wanted to learn something new. He was willing to change his mind. Insight, like a gigantic *yes, of course!* pushes its way to the surface of consciousness, to be received by the learner as a gift, says Lonergan. *It comes in a flash, on a trivial occasion, in a moment of relaxation...not by learning rules, not by following precepts, not by studying any methodology...*[5]

Surprise – what you could call a mismatch between expectation and experience – requires an open mind. The history of science provides us with many dramatic instances of how creative people have kept their questions alive and their imaginations open to new horizons.

For instance, after much research, Darwin was surprised by the theory of natural selection. In his words, *it suddenly flashed upon me.* While working in the patent office, Einstein was surprised to receive *the happiest thought of my life:* a new understanding of how space and time connect in the universe – his general theory of relativity.

To risk learning something new is also to risk a radical change in our self-understanding and in our way of living in the world. While the initial change takes place within, the consequences of new understandings reverberate through our relationships with the people with whom we share our living in the world. We think and act differently because of what we have come to know and this transformation can be unsettling for everyone. The initial joy of discovery can move quickly into a state of anxiety, for instance learning something about a friend that we now wish we didn't know.

Israel Scheffler reflects on what he calls the *epistemological distress* that sometimes follows on new understanding. To be surprised by what we have learned is to find ourselves in a new space, facing unknown horizons and ways of being in the world. The point is that when we take the risk of learning something new the *joy* of what we hoped to discover doesn't automatically follow.

While insight illuminates reality, it can also provoke the discomfort of uncertainty. Insights can conflict with prior beliefs. Skeptics tend to reject the possibility of understanding something new while dogmatists tend to deny the validity of a new understanding that contradicts long-held theories. Consciousness expands or contracts with the questions asked or not asked. The choice is difficult and we often find ourselves thinking: *I don't want to go there so I won't ask the question, even to myself.* Or, *this simply can't be so,* as some people insisted when a man first walked on the moon. To follow through on our questions, even the uncomfortable ones, is to risk the surprise of learning something new, but Scheffler assures us that the risk is worthwhile: *Surprise may be transformed into wonder or curiosity, and so become an educative occasion...if we allow confusion to lead to questioning.*[6]

(3) Insight arises from inner conditions:

The claim that human intelligence can grasp the inner reality (essence) of what *is,* is essential to Lonergan's cognitional theory so the distinction he now makes between mere sensation – what is perceived – and the act of insight or intelligent grasp of a pattern in the data – what is understood – is crucial to our reflection on what we are doing when we come to knowledge. *The occurrence and the content of sensation stand in some immediate correlation with outer circumstance. But with insight internal conditions are paramount.*[7]

What Lonergan is getting at here is the human capacity to get the point of *experience.* Unlike a computer, human intelligence doesn't just absorb information but asks questions such as *what? why?* He says there is a *strange difference between insight and sensation.* The momentum that propels us toward insight includes willingness to become intelligently engaged in a question about the the image suggested by the imagination. What Archimedes perceived (received externally) in the baths of Syracuse was overflowing water. What his intelligence grasped was the *meaning* of the experience (received interiorly). The insight that he achieved was an answer to his question: *why was the water overflowing?* The answer that came to him was an inner act of intelligence: *the weight of his body caused the water to overflow.* Active intelligence moved him from what the senses were feeling (empirical consciousness) to the intelligible pattern in the experience (intellectual consciousness). Even as his body moved in the water, Archimedes grasped this clue: the weight of his body was causing the water to overflow. It was only after he had learned the inner connection between weight and volume that Archimedes ran through the streets telling the world: *I've got it!*

Lonergan describes the three inner conditions required for the achievement of insight:

- The personal awareness of actively engaged intelligence.
- The habitual question why?
- The accurate representation or image of the problem.

Active intelligence is inner because it is the *birth and life in us of the light and evidence by which we operate on our own.* It is the awareness that *we* have grasped what is going on. It is being able to say yes, *I've got it!* not because we are smart or have high scores on I.Q. tests or because we carry in our notebook someone else's words or insights and are able to repeat them. *Active intelligence* is our own inner activity consciously engaged in understanding what's happening around us in the process of creative living and learning.

We are often surprised when it is not there because we have come to expect it. An example:

I used to teach a class each day at one p.m. and was in the habit of going to the cafeteria for a carton of milk and taking it to my desk where I read over my notes as I ate my lunch. Three days in a row, when I got back to my desk – four floors up – I discovered the milk I'd purchased was sour. The third day, in a fluster, I went back downstairs and asked who was responsible for the milk machine.

A young woman behind the counter said, *I am.*

I asked: *Did you know the milk has been sour this week?*

She replied, *My job is to fill the machine, not to know whether it is sour.*

The woman seemed surprised that I expected more. Her natural capacity to question, the habitual *why?* wasn't functioning when she filled the milk machine. She had not gone beyond the level of sensation (empirical consciousness). She missed the connection (intellectual consciousness) between the activity of filling the milk machine and the fact that people actually drank the milk. No *inner conditions* were operating. The lights were out and there was nobody home.

An accurate presentation of the problem provides the image that holds the clue for questions to unpack. The imagination focuses the image of the problem as we puzzle our way to understanding. In a detective story, the image of a page turned down at a certain passage is the clue that triggers a whole set of questions. A clue is only an external sensation until intelligence moves in with the question. When the connection is made, understanding is achieved.

Some years ago, I was exploring with a group of students the role of images and questions in the process of coming to insight. I showed them a video clip from the local news. Two teen aged boys had played a game of dare with a gun at a party and one ended up dead and the other charged with manslaughter. The TV journalist interviewed several young people who were their friends, some of whom had witnessed the tragedy. She asked them *why?* the deadly game might have appealed to the two boys. One of the friends answered: *The excitement of power... to hold a gun must have given him power.* Another friend who was not at the party said that she remembered him as someone always looking for the acceptance of his peers. His father's answer to the journalist's question of why he thought his son would have played the game was: *The too easy availability of a gun.*

The discussion that followed with my students brought to light how an inaccurate image can deflect from an accurate presentation of the problem. The young friends applied their questions to the image of the boy holding the gun to his head. The father of the dead boy, on the other hand, applied his questions to the image of a gun in a storage case. One student wondered if the father of the dead boy was (understandably) refusing to face his son's responsibility for his own tragic choice. This led to a further discussion of the importance of asking the right questions, why we often ask the wrong questions, the courage and stamina it takes to pursue all the questions that arise, and finally the responsibility to accept what we have come to understand when the questions have stopped.

(4) Insight pivots between the concrete and the abstract:

Archimedes wondered about something concrete – King Hiero's crown. His own concrete experience of the bath led him to the answer. Slipping into the water, he grasped the clue that he needed to measure the content of the king's crown. What he grasped, however, was a pattern of intelligibility, an insight that he would express as the abstract law of displacement and specific gravity. The creative insight solved the king's problem, who perhaps wasn't interested in the experience in the bath!

How did this happen? Archimedes had been living with the question of how a crown's content could be measured. His habitually inquiring intelligence pivoted his attention from the concrete experience of the movement of the water to another like-situation and he grasped the abstract principle of volume displacement and specific gravity.

When active intelligence follows through on its dynamic, natural tendency for correction and growth, it cannot stop with concrete experience. Human beings such as my *lobster boy* want more than words. We want to understand the meaning of experience. Lonergan says: *by its very nature insight is the mediator, the hinge, the pivot* connecting the concrete world of sense and imagination with the abstract world of thought or science.[8]

With this image of intelligence pivoting and connecting on a spiral, the usual dichotomy between abstract and concrete dissolves as the whole of what it means to understand is grasped. To achieve insight, the learner moves through a spiraling process from concrete experience toward abstract thought and back again. *It is only at the end of the whole spiraling process (between concrete and abstract) that one has the finished product.*[9]

The 1946 film *The Miracle Worker* tells the story of Helen Keller and her teacher, Ann Sullivan. The film provides a dramatic illustration of a child pivoting on the spiral between the concrete experience of *words* and the abstract *whole* of the function of language. One scene shows the teacher, making word signs for *water* in the child's hand as Helen's other hand holds a pitcher under the pump spilling out water. Keller later would recall the day she learned not just the word-sign for w-a-t-e-r but the whole meaning of language.

I had learned eighteen or twenty words before that thought flashed into my mind, as the sun breaks upon the sleeping world; and in that moment of illumination the secret of language was revealed to me...That word startled my soul...until that day my mind had been like a darkened chamber,

waiting for words to enter and light the lamp, which is thought.[10]

What Keller had grasped was the pattern of relations spiraling between the concrete (words) and the abstract (inner thought about their meaning). This insight gave her the connection between what her teacher had written in her palm and the abstract principle of language representing the meaning of real things. *I knew then that w-a-t-e-r meant the wonderful cool something that was flowing over my hand.*[11]

(5) Insight passes into the habitual texture of one's mind.

Insight transforms the very *being* of the learner in the world. *Before Archimedes could solve his problem, he needed an instant of inspiration. But he needed no further inspiration when he went to offer the king his solution.*[12] His eureka meant he had been changed by what he *got!* There was something different about his way of being-in-the world as he gave his explanation to the king. To understand is to *stand under* or hold within one's grasp the intelligibility of the data before even it is expressed in some external form. Archimedes knew, not just in the folds of his brain but in the luminousness of his own being the solution to the King's problem.

Finally...

When I say *I've got it!* I mean *it's mine!* A story from my early teaching experience, illustrates how children experience and display to the world their basic human capacity to learn for themselves. My classroom was a space under a tree, my students a small group of black seven-year-olds who were happy to be out of the cotton field where their parents worked through the long, hot, Louisiana summe I told the children this story about Jesus, taken from the Bible:

On that day, when evening had come, he said to them, 'Let us go acrc to the other side.' And leaving the crowd behind, they took him with th in the boat, just as he was. Other boats were with him. A great windstc arose, and the waves beat into the boat, so that the boat was already b swamped. But he was in the stern, asleep on the cushion; and they woke up and said to him, 'Teacher, do you not care that we are perishing woke up and rebuked the wind, and said to the sea, 'Peace! Be still!' The

wind ceased, and there was a dead calm. He said to them, 'Why are you afraid? Have you still no faith?' And they were filled with great awe and said to one another, 'Who then is this, that even the wind and the sea obey him?' (Mark 4:35-41)

At the end of the morning, I asked the children if anyone was willing to retell the story to the group. Thomas volunteered and gave us a very dramatic and convincing account of what had happened on the lake.

Jesus was asleep on a pilla in the boat when the waves came up and started rockin the boat...up and down...and the men started yellin' at Jesus: Lawd, save us we drowndin! And Jesus stood up like this in the boat and fussed at them, then he stopped the storm (with arms flailing) an' he 'tole his friends: Whatsa matta with y'all? Ah'm wit y'all. Y'all don't need be skeeered!

There was no doubt in my mind that Thomas had *got it!* He'd understood the point of the story and was able to express his understanding in images, words and concepts that were particularly his own. He wasn't parroting what he had heard about Jesus' power to take away fear. From his own understanding, Thomas had created something new for us.

Though this experience happened many years ago, it remains as a small trophy of my desire not just to teach but to have students learn. And most importantly, to hope with Lonergan, that when we learn how our minds work as we achieve insights, we will become free enough to learn and live creatively as we make our own unique contribution to our world. *For intellectual habit is not possession of the book but freedom from the book. It is the birth and life in us of the light and evidence by which we operate on our own.*[13]

*...when the imagination is prevented from functioning,
the intelligence is prevented from functioning too...*

*Our faculty of understanding...has no capacity whatever
for understanding, not even for understanding the things
from which it abstracts the forms, except by turning to
images.*

Bernard Lonergan, Collection

*Whatever is given
Can always be reimagined, however four-square,
Plank-thick, hull-stupid and out of its time
It happens to be.*

Seamus Heaney, The Settle Bed

3. Imagination – hinders or helps creative learning and living

At the end of their day in the public school, the Mexican-American children of Clifton, Arizona, came to an old building near the Catholic church for religious instruction. Because the fourth-grade children were *mine* for only one hour each week, I anticipated every minute of our time together, planning activities that would get their attention and draw them into the lesson.

One day, when the word *worship* was the focus of the lesson, I began by showing slides I assumed would evoke feelings of wonder and awe. Just a few weeks before, the same children had been captivated by the Bible story of Moses and the burning bush.

I didn't have to look far for material that would evoke awe – or so I believed. Clifton is a small town (population about 600) nestled between two towering mountains, near the Phelps-Dodge open-pit copper mine in Morenci, Arizona. I lived in a trailer house on the side of the mountain and every time I opened the front door and looked up I was moved to wonder. The sheer bulk of the naked rock, the variety of colors from morning's burnished bronze to evening's delicate purple, the golden poppies that claimed their space in the rock crevices to offer their beauty to the world, moved me to gratitude.

I asked a geologist who worked at the mine how the copper got there. He was delighted with my question and brought me outside to the school yard. There he used the sand and rocks to re-enact the way molten lava passes from the center of the earth on its way to become solid veins of copper embedded in the mountain. He explained how the men who came to work there every day hacked it out of the mountain, melted it down in the smelter and produced the large copper bars that were transported all over the world. I should have grasped a clue here but I didn't.

Instead, I showed the children a series of picture-slides of the mountains. Confident of their response, I followed with these questions: *What do you see? How does the mountain make you feel? When you listen, what does the mountain say to you?* The answers were not what I expected: *That's where my Dad works – It makes me feel sad – I hear my Dad yelling at my Mom when he comes home – she makes us go outside.*

Clearly, my awe-inspiring mountain wasn't available to them. They were not at all moved by the beauty that was there. Why not? People came from around the world to look at these mountains. I went home that day disappointed and sad that I hadn't been able to share my own mountain experience with the children. What had *I* missed?

The fathers of the children had felt brutalized by *their* experience of the mountain. That's what I had missed. The men who labored long hours in 23 day cycles in desperate working conditions felt like victims. They understandably resented the power of the company that controlled their lives even as it paid them good wages. The children had absorbed the feeling of helplessness permeating their home life. It had been naive of me to presume that my mountain experience would carry the same meaning for them. I was a beginning teacher at the time, but the question that arose out of the experience became a constant in my own teaching practice: What to do with the feeling tone that students bring to the learning process?

Years later, reading Lonergan's explanation of *dramatic bias,* I came to understand *why* the children's capacity to experience the mountain as an object of beauty had been blocked. The patterned feelings or images that censor experience also limit the capacity to make sense or meaning of it. It was the patterned feelings of their life at home that had prevented the children of Clifton from learning what I wanted to teach them. Images hindered the freedom that would have allowed them to be open to the new experience of the mountain that I offered them. Because they couldn't imagine something different, they were not free to learn for themselves. Common sense intelligence, Lonergan says, can be inhibited by unconscious blindness – *scotosis* – that acts as a censor to the imagination and prevents insight from happening because...*the materials that emerge in consciousness are already patterned, and the pattern is already charged emotionally.*[1]

Now as I prepare classes for university students, my experience with the children of Clifton, Arizona has become a neon sign blinking in my brain: *IMAGINATION! IMAGINATION! IMAGINATION!*

images come to consciousness...

Paying attention to experience, even the ordinary experience of sharing a story, helps us to recognize how emotionally charged images actually affect our capacity to learn from life-experience.

Flannery O'Connor's short story *Everything that Rises Must Converge*, illustrates what I mean. O'Connor herself has said that she uses *three sensuous whacks* to make something real for the reader. Her characters leap off the page and draw us into the drama of their ordinary living. In the story, a mother and son living in the deep South, ride a bus to town in the early days of public integration. The reader is given a vivid impression of the various characters through feelings and images that emerge as black passengers board and Julian's mother (who doesn't seem to have a name of her own) relates to them in her usual *uppity* white manner. Julian is a college graduate and imagines himself to be more intelligent and accepting than his mother of the changes in their world. The mother seems stuck in the past: *her eyes, sky-blue, were as innocent and untouched by experience as they must have been when she was ten.* The dramatic tension builds as a black woman and a small boy get on the bus. Julian laughs to himself because the woman is wearing the same ridiculous (he thinks) purple velvet hat as his mother. When they get off the bus at the same stop, Julian's mother reaches into her pocketbook and gives the black child a penny. The child's mother reacts to the gesture in rage and punches Julian's mother in the face, knocking her to the ground. After he helps her up, Julian decides his mother might as well be made to understand what has happened to her. *Don't think that was just an uppity Negro woman, he says, that was the whole colored race which will no longer take your condescending pennies. That was your black double....What all this means is that the old world is gone. The old manners are obsolete and your graciousness is not worth a damn.* O'Connor ends the story with a shocking tragedy. Her intended meaning is conveyed in the image of the identical purple hat worn by both women. All that rises has converged – and even Julian loses his own mask of superiority – he is human just like everybody else.[2]

Stories don't tell us what to do or what to think or how to measure ourselves against a norm but they do give us a safe place to roam and to wonder. Because the O'Connor story evokes a variety of responses (e.g. some students siding with the mother and others with the son) it illustrates how each person in the room, as well as each character in the story brings a unique pattern of already emotionally charged images to the experience. As students reflect on their own experience of the story and listen to others do the same, they begin to relax into learning for themselves.

An excerpt from an essay about the personal experience to which he had paid attention illustrates how one student was able to identify both the images that arose in consciousness and the questions that surfaced.

*The **experience** I had was at a concert in early September, a few days after I had gotten back to the city after working on a farm all summer. The band was called 'Godspeed You Black Emperor' and I can best describe their style using words like apocalyptic, post-industrial, dark, hopeful, classically-influenced, trance-rock. But the type of music playing is not the point.*

One of the things that crossed my mind during the show was that I was witnessing the 'greatest triumph of humanity.' This was probably a result of discussing the Deep Blue-Kasparov article in class. (The article was about a panel of experts raising questions about a chess match between a computer named Deep Blue and the chess champion.)[3]

What was going on in the concert hall was not only a mechanical (musical) masterpiece comparable to the chess game but also a very high level of communication happening both between performers and between the performers and the audience.

*The **image** that I use to refer to my experience of that night is a dark concert hall where about a thousand Montreal freakish folks are completely entranced. This is a **list of some questions** going through my head since that night: Is this the self indulgence of city life, just like going to movies, school, hanging out at cafes, looking at art? (remember, I had just been on a farm for four months). I love it, but I don't feel balanced doing only this. The experience is similar in a strange way to my experiences of wilderness. Going to wilderness is much the same – a self-indulgent experiencing of pure nature, yet without any notions of having a dependence on the physical world which one is experiencing as an observer. When we are so removed from what sustains us, do we require extreme experience to know we are alive, like rock climbing and going to smoky concert halls? I am amazed that this one event, a concert, has become a symbol for me of my understanding of the world, and I am sure the image of it will remain a reference for a long time.* (Kevin Walsh)

Kevin is typical of those students who have become attentive to the workings of their own minds as they experience their own unique images and questions arising in consciousness. They are ready to consider a variety of theories or explanations of how the imagination functions in creative learning and living. We explore the next question with the help of some poets, scientists and philosophers.

the human imagination at work...

Ted Hughes, the late British poet laureate, explains the function of the imagination as a *faculty of creating a picture of something in our heads and holding it there while we think about it*.[4] He believes that the imagination is a valuable piece of practical mental equipment because it is the control panel for everything we think and do. He says that educators should learn to mine its value because it is the best resource available to help students learn for themselves. Hughes describes three degrees of imagination.

A person of *no imagination* who functions rigidly, works on precedent, principles and orders because (unconsciously perhaps) she/he thinks that something or someone cannot change. A person of *inaccurate imagination* overlooks or misinterprets what is there and wears blinkers to keep out what is undesirable. A person of *accurate and strong imagination* integrates the outer aspects of human experience, sharp, clear, objective perceptions, with inner aspects that are intuitive, incoherent and subjective. This person tunes into experience by means of the delicate wiring of inner awareness and an outer, sensitive antennae.

Persons of *strong imagination* have access to the delicate wiring of artistic consciousness and the sensitive antennae of attentive perception to integrate the outer and inner worlds in their creative work. Says Hughes: *these works seem to heal us...humanity is truly formed...it (the connection) has to be done again and again. The inner world separated from the outer world is a place of demons. The outer world separated from the inner world is a place of meaningless objects and machines.*[5]

David Bohm, one of the great physicists of the twentieth century, describes the imagination *as a power to display the activity of the mind as a whole through mental images.*[6]

In a collection of essays named *On Creativity*, Bohm warns the reader that scientific theories tell us how human *minds* understand the world, they don't tell us how the world really *is*. To believe otherwise is to put blinkers on our capacity to imagine *new* understandings of how the world works and to cut off the continuing human conversation about knowledge. He uses the image of a charged electro-magnetic field to explain how the scientific imagination functions in the learning process. The energy and ordering activity of the mind arises as tension between two poles similar to that generated by an electrical field. *Every mental process must contain the two sides of insight and fancy together, though in each particular step there may be more emphasis on one side or the other.*[7]

The primary or creative imagination – the *fancy* pole – is what generates images and questions and scientific discoveries that tell us something new about the world, says Bohm. The secondary imagination – the *insight* pole – displays the mind's activity of mechanically reconstructing or re-arranging images and insights and concepts already available to the memory.

The tendency of some scientists to over-use the secondary (mechanical) imagination to the exclusion of primary (creative imagination) inhibits the learning process, says Bohm. Nothing new is learned if questions are limited by a rigid boundary of already formulated scientific concepts, no matter how creatively re-arranged. Scientists who work complacently in the world of the *already known* horizon, with the purpose only of verifying their findings to others should, says Bohm, take courage and expand their horizon of inquiry into the world of the creative imagination. The scientific world of our time needs to discover the unknown realm of *what if.*

Since David Bohm said his theory of the imagination was inspired by his reading of the romantic poet Samuel Taylor Coleridge (1772-1834) I was curious to learn more about Coleridge's explanation of the function of imagination.[8]

Coleridge described the function of imagination, not as *poles* of electrical charges, but as primary and secondary *degrees* of reality. The primary imagination is *the living power and prime agent of all human perception, a repetition in the finite mind of the eternal act of creation in the infinite I AM.* The secondary imagination is *an echo of the former, coexisting with the conscious will. It dissolves, diffuses, dissipates, in order to recreate, it struggles to idealize and to unify.*[9] For Coleridge, the primary imagination is the gift of symbolic utterance given to all humans to connect with the divine. It represents the human mind working to its fullest capacity. The secondary imagination is described as a more specialized version of the primary imagination in which artistic consciousness dismantles the world of perception and creates things anew.

Coleridge wrote about the function of the imagination, apparently, as a way of understanding and validating the poet's craft. The aim of poetry, he said, was to facilitate communion with the sacred element in all of life. He uses the language of religion – in his time he had no other – to critique the success or failure of the poem. For him, the mark of the poet's success was the poem's ability to draw readers into a heightened awareness of their own union with the divine Creator.

James Joyce would later describe the artist as a kind of *priest* of the imagination bringing experience and consciousness together in what he called an *epiphany*. A 'showing' to others of the reality perceived by the artist, deeper than ordinary appearances and revealed to the world by means of the artist's creative act. Coleridge recognized in the poetry of Wordsworth this same kind of original, fresh, creative perception expressed in images and words. This was the human equivalent of divine creation that he named *spots in time...such moments, worthy of all gratitude, scatter'd everywhere.* For Coleridge, the primary imagination has access to the whole of reality including the divine. In his explanation, the poet's *symbolic utterance* becomes the breath of God revealing that the divine has discovered *us* and makes claims on us.[10]

For Coleridge, the vehicle of the human connection with the divine Creator is the work of the imagination – and only the imagination. The *imagination* is the active agent, the lens and filter of the mind's desire to connect with the real.

Lonergan situates *our native orientation to the divine* within human intelligence, which he names *the spark in our clod* that stretches us toward the whole of reality.[11] However, intelligence cannot function without the work of the imagination, because, says Lonergan:

...when the imagination is prevented from functioning, the intelligence is prevented from functioning too...Our faculty of understanding...has no capacity whatever for understanding, not even for understanding the things from which it abstracts the forms, except by turning to images.[12]

In Lonergan's cognitional theory, imagination suggests or presents the pattern of intelligibility in a singular sensible form (the phantasm or image). *Intelligence*, the active power of the mind (the agent) then pivots between the concrete (image) and the abstract (form) and *grasps* the meaning or intelligibility of the sensible pattern. In other words, in Lonergan's scheme, intelligence and imagination must *collaborate* in the learning process.[13]

Because Coleridge's explanation of the imagination lacks epistemological refinement, it is often dismissed by those who assume that imagination has little to do with *real* knowledge. True, he places intellect, will and memory, symbols, metaphor and images all under the aegis of the imagination. Coleridge's explanation of how *symbolic utterance* ushers us into the deep encounter with reality strikes a chord with Lonergan's explanation of the collaborative work of intelligence and imagination on the way to knowledge of the real.

The imagination, working at its highest pitch, creates the symbolic world where the deepest encounter can take place... It is the special character of symbol that it is able to usher us into this world without taking away the mystery. Symbol reveals the deepest mysteries of human life, but respects their ultimate resistance to revelation. Symbol leaves the mysteries as it find them – awesome, compelling, radiant with darkness and with light.[14]

A story of my own experience provides an instance of how *the mysteries* are revealed in ordinary events of human lives. Once, I was with a group of people who had come to the funeral service of a very old monk who had lived in a state of extreme dementia for the last twenty years of his life. Standing at his open grave, I found myself asking the question that often beats at the walls of my own consciousness: *What was the meaning of this particular life?* My thoughts were heavy and dark as the coffin was lowered into the grave. A prayer committing him back to the earth and asking angels to come and guide him to his final home offered little light. Then, suddenly, a monarch butterfly appeared. It must have had a wingspan of six inches – all orange and black in design and shimmering with life. It swooped down and made three imperious rhythmical dives into the grave before flying away out of sight. I looked around and saw a few people smiling; others seemed not to notice. My own heart was pounding. The answer to my question came in the *symbolic utterance* of the flight of the butterfly leading and drawing me into the mystery.

biases hinder the work of the imagination...

Insights are kept at bay by *biases*, says Lonergan. Biases are like blinkers suppressing those images that would suggest intelligible patterns of understanding. More than fifty years ago Lonergan described the *tumor of our age* as a collective *flight from understanding.*

Besides the love of light, there can be a love of darkness...To exclude an insight is also to exclude the further questions that would arise from it, and the complementary insights that would carry it towards a rounded and balanced viewpoint.[15]

In his lecture on *Healing and Creating in History* Lonergan asks: *Why are the multinationals permitted to do what they do?* Because, he answers: *the wheel of progress becomes a wheel of decline when the process is distorted by bias. And the situation becomes the dump in which are heaped up...all the biases of self-centered and shortsighted individuals and groups.*

Freedom of consciousness – the *recreation of the liberty of the subject* – allows questions and insights and more questions and more insights to arise. *Insights can be implemented only if people have open minds... insights will not be grasped and implemented by biased minds.*[16]

What Lonergan means by *biased minds* is explored in *Insight* in chapters six and seven on common sense intelligence. There, he describes psychic or neurotic bias; individual or egoistic bias; group or collective egoism bias; general or common sense bias.[17]

Neurotic bias functions on the unconscious level, usually initiated by the experience of a major emotional trauma that overwhelms the psyche and blocks the spontaneous process of learning. Neurotic bias thrives on the fear of understanding something that would alter one's self-image or one's way of life. It creates blind spots or sore spots that remain unconscious but manage to come up through the cracks to block those images that are just too painful to unpack with questions. Neurotic bias avoids pain by replacing the pain-causing image with another less-painful image and affect.

This story of a university student who was taking a course on the spiritual life of children illustrates the power of neurotic bias. When he was five years old, this young man was told that his newborn brother was still in the hospital even though the baby had already died. Left to his own imaginings, he began to feel resentful towards the baby for disrupting his life and taking his parents away from home and from him. He learned of his brother's death months later because he overheard his grandmother speaking to his mother about the dead child. His next experience with someone dying occurred when he was told of his grandmother's death. He was now a teenager and he experienced this news with a feeling of fear so overwhelming that he refused to go to the funeral.

For their first assignment in this class, I had asked students to have a conversation with a child under 10 about their thoughts on where they were before they were born and where they thought they were going after this life. I hoped they would discover something about the "spiritual" life of children through the images already there in the grooves of their imagination. Students were expected to write a report on what they had learned from the child. This was when 'Angelo' came to me in a state of panic, saying he couldn't do this assignment. The thought of death made him sweat and paralyzed his brain, he said. He couldn't understand his reaction. Angelo, a star on the basketball team, very macho Italian, was reduced to tears at the thought of listening and learning something about death and life from a child.

It took a few conversations and some intense image work, but eventually he came to understand that his irrational fear of learning something new emerged from a long-ago memory of resentment toward his brother. Added to this was the mistaken, but emotionally charged image of himself having contributed to the baby's death. Once he replaced the mistaken image with one of himself as a child who could not have been responsible for his brother's death, the fear also moved away.

Individual bias – refuses the free-play of inquiry and interferes with the work of intelligence by restricting possible questions to one's own interest. The egoist is intelligent, cunning even, but limited by the bias of a preoccupation with oneself. Questions that would interfere with one's own interest or concern are prevented from arising.

Egoistic bias operates for instance in class discussions when one student raises his hand before another has finished speaking. The raised hand becomes a dam holding back entrance to other viewpoints that might arise by listening and giving free rein to more questions of one's own. Even when actually engaged in this kind of discussion about individual bias inhibiting learning, the hand-raiser usually doesn't get it! Unlike pre-conscious neurotic bias, individual bias is the result of a conscious choice to narrow the horizon of experience/ feeling/ image/ questions/ insights/ to one's own interest and concern. It is a conscious choice against the light of understanding. *Operative within him there is the desire and drive to understand; he gives it free rein where his own interests are concerned; yet he will not grant serious consideration to its further relevant questions.*[18] In my academic career, I have participated in a number of departmental meetings that are wonderful examples of this kind of individual bias gone mad!

Group bias is egoistic bias expanded to the interest of the group. No good comes from a group that is attentive only to what will benefit itself. A collective blind spot, much like an individual blind spot, keeps questions from arising that would possibly lead to understanding and progress. When the ethos and interests of a particular group dominate a community instead of meeting the needs of the whole, progress is stopped and group bias contributes to decline. This bias is operative when questions that could lead to an insight that wouldn't serve the interests of the dominant group, are excluded. For instance, the effectiveness of a particular group's style of leadership has come to an end, but the questions that would bring this into open dialogue and bring something new to the group are not allowed.

In one phase of my life, I served on the Commission for Religious Education which was part of the Canadian Conference of Catholic Bishops. For three years, I was part of a team of catechists working on the revision of the Canadian catechism used throughout Canada. Our creative-writing process included the distribution of draft versions of lessons to teachers all over the country to try them out on children and give us feedback. The final version of the three already published programs included the valuable input of about a hundred teachers in the field.

Then the bishops informed the writing team that they had decided to eliminate the piloting of the next year's religion program. The thirty lessons that were destined for teachers to try out would instead be sent directly to press. It soon became clear that the reason for this decision was money. The Bishops Conference needed money *now* for some of its projects and the publication and sale of the next year's catechism would meet this need. The members of the writing team strenuously objected to the decision and the way it had been made without consulting the people who had done all the work. When the presiding bishop responded to our objections by leaning across the table and saying *trust me*, I heard: 'Don't ask any more questions/let me decide what would be good for the group.' The meeting ended on this note. The following week the writing team was disbanded and replaced by another group of people who accepted the decision without question. The un-piloted program went to press. The interests and bias of the dominant group had prevailed.

General bias is the bias of common sense itself seeking short term and immediate solutions to complex problems. Since common-sense intelligence has no theoretical aspirations and is action-driven, its own practicality can get in the way of learning from experience. For instance, it might dismiss the "vision thing" as irrelevant to current problems and relegate the consideration of the whole picture to people who are paid to "think" but not to make policy decisions about "real" life. General bias would solve the problem *now* with the means at hand and exclude any questions that would lead to a long-term view, questions such as: *What is the cause of the problem? How can we prevent it from happening again? Will this action cause more and bigger problems down the road?*

Common-sense intelligence says what it· means to someone, hopes for a response in the listener, has no theoretical aspirations, does not use technical language or formal modes of speech, and does not aim for exhaustive communication. All this is fine when attending to concrete problems that need immediate solutions. However, to eliminate critical reflection on the long-term view eliminates as well the functioning imagination that would suggest images of new possibilities that offer hope that tomorrow can be different from today. People infected with common sense bias never allow themselves to imagine *what if?* Instead, says Lonergan, they live aimlessly in the realm of senseless routine, asking despairingly, what can *I* do?

Finally...

We are bombarded with images from morning to night. To come to our own understanding of how the imagination functions and how biases put blinders on the desire to know, lets the learner know what to do to re-appropriate the basic human capacity to know what is real. The ideal of knowledge that Lonergan suggests: *myself as intelligent, as asking questions, as requiring intelligible answers,* assumes the collaboration of imagination and intelligence.[19] The most characteristic mental trait of humankind, Susanne Langer claims, is the freedom to abstract from sense data (image) and to express symbolically what has been intelligently grasped. Only humans, she says, have the freedom (power) of *regarding everything about a sense-datum as irrelevant except a certain form that it embodies.*[20] A strong and accurate imagination, says Ted Hughes, is the teacher's best resource to help students learn for themselves.

We live in a world without hope. Most of us are not sure that we matter in the bigger picture or that the world might need what we have to give. Margaret Visser, in her book *Beyond Fate,* recognizes in contemporary culture, a pattern of slipping back into the fatalistic thinking of the Greeks whose lives were *fated,* to be lived within controlling lines *(moira)* drawn by the gods. Institutional bureaucracy, economic determinism, advertising and the media are some of the "gods" that seem to draw the controlling lines around our lives today. Absent from this horizon is the vertical or transcendent dimension of human life where people use their imagination to *search for better models for human existence, where they struggle towards liberation.*[21] By re-appropriating the capacity of our own minds to re-imagine our lives, we re-claim the freedom that the "gods" would deny us to better express what it means to be human today. Richard Kearney, in his book, *The Wake of Imagination, says:*

One of the greatest paradoxes of contemporary culture is that at a time when the image reigns supreme, the very notion of a creative human imagination seems under mounting threat. We no longer appear to know who exactly produces or controls the images which condition our consciousness.[22]

We need new symbols to express the religious consciousness of our times. In a talk given in 1965, Lonergan responded to the criticism that his thought was too cerebral with these words: *the human spirit expresses itself in symbols before it knows, if ever it knows, what its symbols literally mean.*[23]

The fact that we spontaneously turn to the imaginative mode of expression to articulate the deeper experiences of human living tells us how we already know that symbols offer shelter for what we cannot seem to understand or express adequately. Affect-charged images or symbols expand consciousness and allow us to dwell consciously in the presence of the ineffable mystery that is called "God."[24] I am convinced that the people who flock to the sites where human tragedy has happened, leaving flowers and cards and lighting candles, articulate a deep and old human wisdom. Symbols and rituals, not reasons or logic, achieve the psychic transformation that the human spirit needs to re-imagine the possibility of goodness in human life and to get on with it. The experience of transcendence in human living always comes as a surprise. It is received as gift – grace – that precedes knowledge. The work of the creative imagination is either preparation or response.

Our deepest fear is not that we are inadequate. Our deepest fear is that we are powerful beyond measure. It is our light, not our darkness, that frightens us most. We ask ourselves, who am I to be brilliant, gorgeous, talented and fabulous?

Actually, who are you not to be? You are a child of God. Your playing small doesn't serve the world. There is nothing enlightened about shrinking so that other people won't feel insecure around you. We were born to make manifest the glory of God within us.

It is not just in some of us; it's in everyone. And, as we let our own light shine, we unconsciously give other people permission to do the same. As we are liberated from our own fear our presence automatically liberates others.

Nelson Mandela

4. Creativity and Consciousness – the creative self comes to be

If the collaboration of imagination and intelligence frees students to engage in their own learning, what can Lonergan's explanation of the spiraling levels of human consciousness contribute to the process? How can students *learn* to express their unique way of *being* in the world?[1]

the creative self comes to be...

Cezanne, who spent years copying the great masters in the Louvre, said that it was a heightened consciousness of the world around him that inspired him to radically change the form of his painting from imitation to impression. Einstein, too, rejected the version of the world he was given at school to follow through on his own child-like questions: Does this thing named *ether* really hold the cosmos together? How does gravity work?

Creative people tune into life and twiddle with the boundaries of inherited tradition to express their unique consciousness of experience. They are not only the talented elite in a culture. Rather they are the risk-takers who have acquired the freedom of imagination and consciousness to move beyond the cultural conditioning and patterns of learning that inhibit the discovery of unexpected answers. Creative people re-imagine what life has given.

The inevitability of form in human discourse dictates that when we pay attention to life experience, listen to the questions that beat at the walls of our consciousness, and wait for insights to arise, we will be driven to express what we have come to understand. Days, months or even years may pass between the life experience that evokes a question, the insight that grasps the tentative answer and the discovery of some creative form that expresses adequately what we have come to understand.

The movement of the human spirit toward creative expression is spontaneous but not automatic. The search for an adequate word or gesture or sign proceeds at a slow, uphill pace. For instance, Emily Carr's experience of Victorian art forms and the art education she received contrasted with her visceral experience of Native art forms and spawned the questions that led her to develop a bolder, more direct style of expression. She made many trips into the primal forests of British Columbia and to the Indian coastal settlements. Carr's grasp of the pulsing flow of life around her inspired a unique form of painting that would become her signature. This came only after a difficult fifteen-year fallow period when she ran a boarding house to make a living and painting became something she did in her spare time. In fact, she felt that *all the art (was) being smashed out of me flat.* Yet the initial questions and insights that inspired her search for an adequate form to express what she had come to understand about the world survived and eventually flourished into her creative living and working. (Interestingly, her painting was initially ignored in Canada until it gained recognition at the Tate Gallery in London.)[2]

Erik Erikson says the creative person has no choice when life questions arise.

He may come across his supreme task almost accidentally. But once the issue is joined, his task proves to be at the same time intimately related to his most personal conflicts, to his superior selective perception, and to the stubbornness of his one-way will: he must court sickness, failure, or insanity, in order to test the alternative whether the established world will crush him, or whether he will disestablish a sector of this world's outworn fundaments and make a place for a new one.[3]

Ideally, education engages students within a given tradition of culture, language, meaning and values and facilitates their critical appropriation of that tradition in a way that makes it accessible to the students of each new generation. Educators who embody this ideal will honor students' experience and questions with a teaching strategy that gives first place to what Bernard Lonergan names the *re-creation of the liberty of the subject.* In other words, when students are free to tune into their own lived experience, to ask their own questions and to express in words or gestures or signs what *they* have understood for themselves, creative selves come to be. Says Lonergan:

> *At any time in any place what a given self can make of himself is some function of the heritage or sediment of common meanings that come to him from the authentic or unauthentic living of his predecessors and his contemporaries.*[4]

Both James Joyce and Bernard Lonergan, each in his own way, have shed light on how the creative self comes to be. James Joyce (1882 -1941) tuned into life in early 20th century Ireland and beyond, played with the boundaries of an inherited classical tradition of learning and created a unique expression of what he had come to understand. How did Joyce do it? By consciously paying attention to his own life experience, by asking his own questions and by risking radical new forms of expression to articulate what he had come to understand.

In *A Portrait of the Artist as a Young Man,* the character of Stephen Dedalus rejects what he names the *dull-witted serf* mentality of Irish culture and writes out of his own experience of life in Dublin. Readers of Joyce's published work recognized themselves in the characters he created, and most of them didn't like who they met. To escape the psychic paralysis that had dulled their day-to-day existence in Ireland, Joyce's early readers would have had to follow his example by re-imagining what was given and re-creating themselves.

> *I will not serve that in which I no longer believe whether it call itself my home, my fatherland or my Church: and I will try to express myself in some mode of life or art as freely as I can and as wholly as I can, using for my defense the only arms I allow myself to use – silence, exile and cunning.*[5]

Joyce's self-imposed exile from Ireland was both an escape from the nets of home, country and religion and his birth-flight into a world of creative learning and living. His willingness to risk all for the writing that would become his lifework shimmers through the last pages of *Portrait...* when he has Stephen leaving Ireland with a mother's prayerful blessing: *she prays now...that I may learn in my own life and away from home and friends what the heart is and what it feels. Amen. So be it. Welcome O life! I go to encounter for the millionth time the reality of experience and to forge in the smithy of my soul the uncreated conscience of my race.*[6]

From the *smithy* of his *soul* Joyce did indeed create a new consciousness in which he expressed *the reality of experience* for twentieth century Ireland and beyond. His portrait of Stephen Dedalus, emerged from a luminous intelligence asking questions of his own lived experience of the Ireland of his times and led to this unique expression of what he had come to understand about what happens when the human heart responds to real life as lived. His later creation of Leopold Bloom in *Ulysses* was probably an expression of his desire to learn more about human consciousness.

In the act of creating Stephen Dedalus as a conscious, intelligent artist who could reason and judge and act for himself, Joyce nudged the *uncreated conscience* of Irish culture into heightened self-awareness. He also changed the notion of what a modern writer could do.[7]

I am sure that wherever he is, Joyce is laughing over my shoulder at the suggestion I am now making that he exemplifies Bernard Lonergan's 1959 challenge to educators: *The great task that is demanded if we are to make (life) livable again is the re-creation of the liberty of the subject, the recognition of the freedom of consciousness.*[8] Joyce admitted that his Jesuit teachers had taught him how to use words to reason and judge and act. Still, as he learned to express himself – relying on the inner authority of his own experience and critical appropriation of inherited tradition – he dramatically rejected the Jesuit system of education and the Catholic Church.

Bernard Lonergan also played with the boundaries of a classical tradition of learning. Out of his own experience of an outworn, even medieval system of schooling – heavily reliant on questions and arguments addressed to authorities of the past – Lonergan asked this very modern question: *what do I myself do when I come to know?* As he became aware of himself attending to life experience, moving from questions for understanding to critical reflection and judgment, to responsible decisions, he discovered something new: how the human mind operates as it searches out objective knowledge of reality.[9] His unique gift to the world was to make accessible a method (a normative unfolding pattern) of learning based on the desire of the human spirit spiraling through heightening levels of awareness (consciousness) toward the achievement of knowing for oneself.[10] He expressed the key to creative learning and living (his cognitional theory) in this disarmingly simple imperative: be attentive, be intelligent, be reasonable, be responsible.[11]

Lonergan says that the consciously aware person moves spontaneously from the sensitive realm of images, stories and words embedded in experience, to intelligent questions such as: *what is this? why?* to reasonable judgments about what is real or true, to responsible deliberations and decisions about the value of what is known. In other words, by spiraling through four levels of consciousness: from the level of experience – data gathering – to the level of engaged intelligence – asking questions – to the level of critical reflection – saying yes or no to the sufficiency of data – to the level of responsible deliberation and choice, the creative self comes to be in a life that is a work of art.

Lonergan says that creative learning and living begins by paying attention to experience. It doesn't end there. The creative process is a *long, hard, uphill climb…and the creative task is to find the answers…a matter of insight, not of one insight but of many. Yet, this creative process is nothing mysterious.*[12] Here is a student's account of the beginning of his own creative process:

If you had told me two years ago that I would be living and studying at a university in Montreal, I would have laughed at the idea – even scorned it. But two years ago my life had no dimension; I was drifting from one rooming-house to another, working at jobs that meant nothing to me, and flipping through the channels for a program to occupy my nights, so that I could forget about the day's events. Numb to existence. If the phone rang, I would look at it in fear. I began to ask myself, not as an immediate question but as a kind of slow dawning: What is at stake here? The answer was not 'my soul' or my 'intellectual-well-being' or even 'my physical existence' – all of which were up for grabs. What was at stake was my word. I would not be present when called upon at a crucial moment. I would not be ready to do what was necessary. What must I do to get out of this fix? The first answer, of course, was not to go to university, but to call my father, having no idea what I would say. One thing leads to another. I accepted the invitation, and my days became shaped by meaning. (Michael McDonald)

When students such as Michael become aware (conscious) that their choices have been self-generated, creative learning and living has begun. *He* picked up the phone! Nothing *mysterious*... he is now a learner in the game of *living* instead of remaining a *drifter*. What Michael consciously desired – to be *present* – initiated the choices that followed. It was consciousness that made him intentionally present and freed his imagination to attend to the pulsing flow of his own life.

In Lonergan's words:

We experience to have the materials for understanding; and understanding, so far from cramping experience, organizes it, enlarges its range, refines its content, and directs it to a higher goal. ...Such vertical finality is another name for self-transcendence. By experience we attend to the other, by understanding we gradually construct our world, by judgment we discern its independence of ourselves; by deliberate and responsible freedom we move beyond merely self-regarding norms and make ourselves moral beings.[13]

Faced with young people who have to be reminded to shut down their cell phones and leave their earphones at the door, teachers today must work hard to find the word or gesture or sign that will engage them in the question of understanding how consciousness functions in the creative process.

Consciousness, in Lonergan's scheme, is *not* standing back and *taking a look* as if one were a spectator at the parade of life. He uses words such as awareness, self-presence, intentional, relational, being attentive to the direction of life. He speaks of the *passionateness of being...that underpins and accompanies and reaches beyond the subject... to guide the individuation process from the ego to the self.*[14]

Examples help to illustrate the difference between being a spectator and being *there in the moment.* For instance, an infant in the act of moving the mobile hanging in his crib displays a basic level of consciousness when he becomes aware that he, himself, makes it move, makes a sound with it, or to it, or whatever and delights at his accomplishment. Consciousness is a state of being aware of one's self as agent, not as a self-enclosed, isolated atom, but as a person open and present to the undertow of life in the real world.

consciousness...heightening...

The word *level*, as Lonergan uses it here, is a metaphor for *desire* on the move. Though the following chart has all the weaknesses of any attempt to express visually the levels of consciousness operative in learning and living, it provides students with an image of the process they have already come to recognize in themselves.[15]

LEVELS	WHAT I WANT	MY QUESTIONS	MY TASK
Empirical	Data		Be attentive
Intelligent	Intelligibility	What is it? Why?	Be intelligent
Rational	Truth-Reality	Is it so?	Be reasonable
Moral	Good-Value	What's it worth?	Be responsible

Lonergan has said that the aim of his book *Insight is to issue an invitation to a personal, decisive act...Though I cannot recall to each reader his personal experiences, he can do so for himself and thereby pluck my general phrases from the dim world of thought to set them in the pulsing flow of life.*[16] He expects readers to personally appropriate the operations of their own mind on the move. Not by twisting around to see what is going on in the back of our head, but by becoming aware that we are (1) *experiencing data:* sensing, perceiving, feeling, imagining. (2) *asking questions:* understanding, formulating; (3) *critically reflecting:* gathering evidence, assenting to what is. (4) becoming *responsible decision makers.*

Consciousness heightens as the desire to grasp the meaning of experience moves toward *intelligence in act* asking a question. For instance, a child is moved to ask: *Where has the moon gone? Why?* Evidence that the second level of consciousness has kicked in comes with questions arising. The image of a Slinky comes to mind, activated by the desire of the human spirit and following its seemingly magical movement down the stairs. To wonder about experience, Lonergan says, is to be released from mere sensation or biological extroversion into the realm of intelligent inquiry about meaning, on the way to objective knowledge of reality. *Rational consciousness* propels us from the intelligent grasp of a pattern in the data toward the next level where we *critically* reflect on what has been understood: *Is it so? Is it real? Is it correct?* (Correct as in *accurate*, but based on evidence which can change tomorrow) Consciousness heightens as desire for accurate judgment occurs. There are two aspects of the act of judgment: appropriation and assent. In other words, before making a judgment of whether something is so, I must first ask myself the question that even the most intelligent of computers cannot ask: *Do I have enough evidence?* And then: *Is it reasonable to assent to what I understand? Or is it unreasonable not to make a judgment about what I have come to understand?*

Students usually resist the word judgment because they associate it with an attitude of condescending righteousness that they want no part of. I suspect that this resistance also comes from foggy thinking about how opinions are acceptable but truth-claims are presumptuous. Perhaps there is the fear factor of personal commitment. Once, a student sitting in the back of the room laughed out loud when I introduced Lonergan's distinction between apprehension and assent. When I asked him what he was laughing at he said: *but if I assent, you can hold me to it.* And I said: *Eureka! You got it!* When we have accepted our own capacity for judgment we have already taken to heart two words: *is* and *I*. To use these words in a concrete situation *means* that we must admit (at least to ourselves) that having judged something *is so, I* can now be held responsible for what I have said. With each level of consciousness, more of myself is on the line.

An example: In Montreal in late March a freak snow storm *is* happening outside. As I take in the scene, (gather sufficient evidence) I *know* that I will have to move my car before the snow-removal people arrive or it will be towed. *I* have made a judgment of what *is*.

To avoid making the judgment would be both unreasonable (denying the facts) and irresponsible (I'll get a parking ticket I can't afford).

A clip taken from a video on the life of the physicist Richard Feynman provides another image of the human desire and capacity to know the real. While he was in Washington, as a member of the President's commission to search out the reasons for the explosion of the 1986 Challenger space shuttle, Feynman wonders if the effort to search for the truth is worth it. In a letter to his wife he explains that the evidence gathered by the committee is shrouded by a cloud of unreality. Public relations, rather than what really happened have become the motive for the search. The people responsible for the construction and operation of the space shuttle must always be perceived by the public as having been knowledgeable and efficient. His wife encourages him to continue gathering evidence of his own. He does and concludes that there was a deficiency in the O rings on the craft. This fact had been reported by some engineers, but ignored by the astronauts and the people making the judgment about safety. When the final report is written up, someone in the higher levels of government decides to eliminate this fact. Feynman contests the decision and passionately points out that since the purpose of the report is to answer the question: 'what went wrong?' *all* the evidence should be included. It should be included, he says, because *reality must take precedence over public relations.*

Feynman's story keeps the discussion concrete. As we pivot from the image to the question of how we come to know the real and back again to the image of Feynman pursuing the truth, these words of Lonergan (on the board) keep us on track: *Objectivity is simply the consequence of authentic subjectivity.*[17] Many of the presuppositions that students bring to the discussion of their own capacity for objective knowledge – Dr Phil says there is no such thing as reality, only perception – what is real is not accessible to ordinary people like us – he must be right, he has a degree from Harvard – gradually dissolve. Students come to recognize in themselves both the desire and the capacity to search for and find objective answers to their questions about the world.

Judgment has proved to be the most difficult aspect of Lonergan's cognitional theory to teach. My fear is to oversimplify what is not simple. My hope is that students will come to understand for themselves that the appropriation of their capacity to make judgments of what is real is a defining moment in the *becoming* of their own authentic creative selves. The human capacity for critical reasoning and reflective judgment is what re-creates the liberty of the subject. Says Lonergan:

...we are not responsible for our memory; we feel no embarrassment if we cannot remember...memory is not completely under our control. But the judgment is a personal act, a personal commitment. You do not have to say yes or no; you can say, 'I don't know'...All the alternatives relevant to human weakness, ignorance, and tardiness are provided for, and it is your rationality that is involved in picking out the right one. Judgment is something that is entirely yours; it is an element in personal commitment in an extremely pure state...it is entirely one's own responsibility.[18]

Since the personal act of judgment is what *transforms a proposition from an object of thought into an object of knowledge,* the achievement of knowledge can never be someone else's work.[19] Understanding, not certainty, puts us on the path to knowledge. When new evidence appears on the horizon, a similar response of critical reflection and judgment of the new data is called for.

Consciousness of our own ability to move beyond mere perception to judgments of fact also reveals the truth that to be human is to be both limited and capable of transcendence. By following through on our *disinterested desire to know* we learn to differentiate between what we assent to in the act of judgment, our own limited grasp of reality, and the *whole* of reality drawing us on and keeping us open to the more. *...the reason why we know is within us...the intellectual light which is in us is nothing other than a participation in the eternal light.*[20]

Lonergan's claim is that the appropriation of our selves as knowers frees us from the tyranny of unrevisable certitudes that paralyses consciousness and inhibits the personal response to received tradition that will keep it alive. This excerpt from a student's essay says it well:

The main way in which my creative process has changed is in my ability to talk about it. Much of the language used by Lonergan was familiar to me before I began the course, but never had it been 'strung together' in a way that made sense, or that I felt I could apply to my own life. I have been able to identify where I am within the learning process – experiencing, understanding, reflecting, or acting upon. Secondly, I am able to talk about it with other people...It is helping me define what it is that I want to get out of my education – both formal and informal. Particularly, I realize that what I'm interested in is the link between authenticity and responsibility – how our inherent desire for authenticity manifests itself in the choices we make. (Kevin Walsh)

Students such as Kevin have learned that by responding to their own deepest desire spiraling through these levels of consciousness, and searching for the word or sign or gesture that will express their own unique understanding of life experience, they discover their creative selves coming to be.

Finally...

The Canadian political philosopher Charles Taylor, in his book *Sources of the Self,* says that because the artists among us know best how to articulate their experience of life, they have become the models of what it means to be human for our times. The self understanding of the modern person, he says, *is a being capable of self articulation.* Artists can show us how to retrieve our own lived experience. Taylor claims that questions directing us to decisions of value arise out of attentiveness to our experience and open us to the inner depths of who we are. Before contemporary persons accept the authority of another's version of what is real, says Taylor, they expect the words they hear to resonate with their own personal experience. Taylor says that authors such as Mann or Joyce or Jung *may take us beyond the subjective, but the road to them passes inescapably through a heightened awareness of personal experience.*[21]

This conscious modern self, echoes Lonergan, is an original creation. *Freely the subject makes himself what he is; never in this life is the making finished; always it is still in process, always it is a precarious achievement that can slip and fall and shatter.*[22] Consciousness, the state of being aware of our own self-presence in the flow of life, is the first step in the evolution of the creative self. Artists, says Lonergan, seem to move naturally within the realm of elemental consciousness, grasping spontaneously the symbolic patterning of experience. Symbolic consciousness is a way of attending/questioning/critically reasoning that artists have perfected in their learning and living. We can learn from them how to attend to the movement of life in the moment, without expecting immediate usefulness or an ulterior purpose. Utilitarianism narrows the horizon and cuts off the natural spontaneity of wonder. Artists teach us how to open ourselves to the surprise of discovery. Seamus Heaney says that artists set the world free to have a new go at its business. And if educators would take to heart Lonergan's challenge to re-create the liberty of the subject, then the business of our day would be to teach in such a way that our students become conscious and creative selves engaged in their own learning.

When Lonergan speaks to educators about art in *Topics in Education,* it seems to me he is telling us that we would learn how to free our own imaginations and live more consciously if only we paid attention to how artists organize the sensitive level of experience. Though he doesn't make direct reference to teaching here, he does tell us indirectly what teachers who are also artists contribute to learning. Art is all about cultivating human potential and freedom of consciousness and imagination. The artist can help us explore ways of feeling and perceiving. The artist reveals to us the pattern in the image that we might have missed on our own. Because most artists are not interested in coming to exact or certain knowledge of the world, they open new horizons that introduce us to a fuller or deeper or different experience of concrete living. By offering their creative expressions to the world, their own symbolic apprehension of reality is given to us. Their gift includes an invitation to experience and perhaps come to understand more of the world than we would on our own.

Tad Dunne, a sometimes artist and former student of Lonergan writes: *A good piece of art communicates virtual space in a way that draws the viewer to a beyond, to an anticipated yet unrealized meaning, to the shadow of 'almost' that falls on even our highest achievements.*[23]

We often learn how to view the beyond through the eyes of our students. Once, in an art museum in New Orleans I found myself following a group of seven year olds being guided by their teacher from one painting to another. I stood behind the children as they sat in front of a large canvas covered with what looked to me to be a big blob of formless light green paint. Then the teacher asked the children: *How does this painting make you feel?* A spirited black boy answered: *JAZZ!*

In the clutter of life, teachers run interference for us by selecting images that evoke questions that lead to personal understanding and eventually knowledge of reality. Lonergan says: *There is an artistic element in all consciousness, in all living. Our settled modes have become humdrum, and we may think of all our life simply in terms of utilitarian categories. But in fact the life we are living is a product of artistic creation. We ourselves are products of artistic creation in our concrete living, and art is an exploration of potentiality.*[24]

You cannot tell what the good is going to be, because the good is not any systematic entity. The good is a history.

Bernard Lonergan, *Topics in Education*

Just as the existential subject freely and responsibly makes himself what he is, so too he makes himself good or evil and his actions right or wrong.

The good subject, the good choice, the good action are not found in isolation. For the subject is good by his good choices and good actions.

Universally prior to any choice or action there is just the transcendental principle of all appraisal and criticism, the intention of the good. That principle gives rise to instances of the good but those instances are good choices and actions.

However, do not ask me to determine them, for their determination in each case is the work of the free and responsible subject producing the first and only edition of himself.

Bernard Lonergan, *The Subject*

5. Creativity and Values – making of our living a work of art

A ripple of resistance traveled across the room when students learned that the next topic in the course would be the *good*. A brave woman in the back row asked tentatively: *You know what 'the' good is?* I assured her that I didn't know what the good is but what I planned to offer was a guided tour through the process that most of us follow when life poses these questions: *what's it worth? what can I do? what shall I do?*

Lonergan's thought on human values can help us understand what is involved in deliberating, evaluating and making decisions as we create a life for ourselves. His claim is that *the* good is not an abstract concept or principle that philosophers have formulated, or an "out there" scientific fact to be verified, but is the result of concrete responsible choices made by developing human beings. One student expressed it this way: *If we accept ourselves as knowers, free to re-imagine what has been given, willing to change as a result of what we have to come to know, then living becomes the ultimate art form.* (Sarah Etzadi-Ezendi)

coming to know and choose the good...

When Seamus Heaney received the Nobel Prize for Literature in 1995, he included in his acceptance speech a story about a group of working men in Northern Ireland. The story's central image of one man squeezing the hand of another is unpacked as we ask: how do human beings struggle toward the concrete choice of what they have decided is *the* good?

One of the most harrowing moments in the whole history of the harrowing of the heart in Northern Ireland came when a minibus full of workers being driven home one January evening in 1976 was held up by armed and masked men and the occupants of the van ordered at gun point to line up at the side of the road. Then one of the masked executioners said to them, 'Any Catholics among you, step out here.' As it happened, this particular group, with one exception, were all Protestants, so the presumption must have been that the masked men were Protestant paramilitaries about to carry out a tit-for-tat sectarian killing of the Catholic as the odd man out, the one who would have been presumed to be in sympathy with the IRA and all its actions. It was a terrible moment for him, caught between dread and witness, but he did make a motion to step forward. Then, the story goes, in that split second of decision, and in the relative cover of the winter evening darkness, he felt the hand of the Protestant worker next to him take his hand and squeeze it in a signal that said no, don't move, we'll not betray you, nobody need know what faith or party you belong to. All in vain, however, for the man stepped out of the line; but instead of finding a gun at his temple, he was pushed away as the gunmen opened fire on those remaining in the line, for these were not Protestant terrorists but members, presumably, of the Provisional IRA.[1]

Lonergan says that three structural components function in every intentional choice of the human good. We are drawn to *the good* because we want it/we expect it/and because it reveals who we are. He also says the *good always is concrete.*[2] Deep down at the core of our being the concrete good is what we *desire.* (the particular good) As we learn to live with one another, we have come to *expect* the concrete good in those orderly structures that we set up to simplify our living together. (the good of order) Finally, we choose the concrete good that reveals *who we are* when, as autonomous human beings we take a stand or make a judgment about what should be done. (the chosen good of value).

I love to remind students that even though it is not yet noon they have already experienced what Lonergan claims to be the components of the human good: they *desire* an education; they *expect* to find what they want in the structure of the university; and by getting out of bed and showing up for class, the world can see who they *are*: autonomous human beings who have chosen the good of learning.[3]

Desire: We choose the good because we long for it. The deliberation and evaluation preceding the choice is weighted with complexity. Nothing is ever simple.

In Heaney's story, the lone Catholic man standing beside the minibus wanted the good. In his situation he must have been torn between two responses: dread because he feared the men with the guns would kill him, and desire to express his deepest self. *Any Catholics among you, step out here.* The words that thrust him into the struggle to decide what to do. To step out was a choice to affirm his identity as a free human being who was a Catholic. To keep back would preserve his life (or so he thought). The gesture to express the truth of himself may have been spontaneous, but it certainly was not automatic – the reality at stake was life or death. There must have been a fleeting moment of reflection and time to ask the dreadful (in this situation) questions: *What's it worth? What can I do? What shall I do?* before making the decision to put his life on the line.

Expectation: We choose the good because we expect it to be there in the structures of our living with one another. The minibus that the workers boarded was part of a transportation system created by people wanting to organize a good way to get people home at the end of their work day. There must have been a coordinated effort among individual human beings to set this up so that the system wouldn't have to be organized anew every day. We normally count on one another to do our jobs as agreed. The driver's tacit agreement to show up at a certain time to drive the men home was something they could reasonably expect. And they did – until the order broke down.

Order is what we expect to be there in social structures but it is broken down by destructive choices made by free human beings. When the members of the Provisional IRA killed all the Protestants who were on the bus, their free choice unleashed violence in their world.

Heaney describes how over a twenty year period similar choices for violence, created in Ireland a society: *of life waste and spirit waste, of hardening attitudes and narrowing possibilities that were the natural result of political solidarity, traumatic suffering, and sheer emotional self-protectiveness.*[4]

Value: In the very asking of the questions: *what's it worth? what shall I do?* says Lonergan, human freedom is experienced *as the active thrust of the subject terminating the process of deliberation by settling on one of the possible courses of action and proceeding to execute it.*[3] Value is embedded in the choice made at the end of the process of deliberating, evaluating and decision. It is an intentional decision to know and do, not just what pleases us but what is judged worthwhile.

When the Catholic man felt the Protestant worker squeezing his hand he got the unspoken message: *I'll not betray you.* The gesture actualized the Protestant man's freedom even as it communicated to the other man *who he was.* He was free to act or not. He must have felt that fleeting moment of freedom before he made the choice to squeeze the hand – the movement of value expressing the core of himself – *this is who I am.*[6]

Heaney has said that in the months and years that followed, as the story was told and re-told among Catholics and Protestants alike in Northern Ireland and beyond, it became a beacon of hope for all who heard it. It affirms the freedom of the human capacity to choose *the* good.

Over the years, as Lonergan continued to explore the question of how we come to know and choose the good, he expanded his early emphasis on structure and rational decision-making to include more explicitly the role that feelings play in our response to values. In *Method,* he explains how feelings modify our spontaneous response to value in this ascending scale of preferences. *Vital* values have to do with acquiring, maintaining and restoring physical health and well being. Social values have to do with the cooperation required to create and sustain social institutions – educational, political, economic, etc. *Cultural* values have to do with finding meaning in our living and operating within an inherited culture. *Personal* values have to do with what we feel is worth putting our identity as self-transcending persons on the line for – moral self-transcendence. *Religious* values have to do with ultimate meaning or the feelings that inform the values that operate at the heart of human existence.[7]

In Insight...the good was the intelligent and reasonable. In Method the good is... intended in questions for deliberation: Is this worthwhile? Is it truly or apparently good? It is aspired to in the intentional response of feeling to values. It is known in judgments of value made by a virtuous or authentic person with a good conscience.[8]

an authentic person with a good conscience...

Mark Twain in his *Adventures of Huckleberry Finn*, tells the story of Huck's interior struggle for authenticity after he has helped his friend, the runaway slave Jim, escape from his owner. Huck suffers from a full blown attack of what he calls *conscience* because he made the choice to help his friend. His inherited culture tells him that a slave is someone's property so he must be a thief. Faced with another choice to *live* with his choice, and deliberating over the consequences, Huck asks himself if the right thing to do in this case would be to give back what was stolen. Deep down (where his conscience is) he knows that in this case what society has judged to be the *right* thing is not the *good* thing. He says to himself: *You can't pray a lie.* So, he chooses the *good* that he knows – friendship. His external programming tells him to choose the *right* thing. But the deeper feeling of who he perceives himself to be – a trusted friend to Jim – directs him to the decision. He will not turn Jim in. Consciousness has become conscience. And he will live with the consequences.[9]

Huck's decision takes him beyond the satisfaction he would feel by gaining social approval. Ultimately it confirms – as his attack of conscience makes clear – his own freedom to transcend mere satisfaction for value. His identity – who he is at the secret core of his being – is influenced but not determined from outside. The chosen good (value), says Lonergan, originates not in the social structures of a particular culture or religion, but in the vigilant willingness of free persons deliberating, evaluating and eventually choosing to make responsible decisions.[10]

Terminal values are the values that are chosen; true instances of the particular good, a true good of order, a true scale of preferences regarding values and satisfactions. Correlative to terminal values are the originating values that do the choosing: they are authentic persons achieving self-transcendence by their good choices.[11]

good choices...

Responding to the deepest core of his being, making a judgment to act on who he really is, Huck not only helps us to understand what a good conscience is but he provides an example of an authentic person transcending the satisfaction of making the "right" choice to make the "good" choice. He follows through on the undertow of feeling that takes him beyond the desire for what is immediately satisfying (what people expect of him) to the choice to act on what he knows to be the real and *the* good. The choice to transcend self satisfaction and to act responsibly can be as simple as not eating the donut we know is bad for our health, or as dramatic as pushing a child out of the way of a dangerous vehicle.

When we find ourselves being responsible, it usually means we are *feeling* an imperative – an inner command – to act on an accepted value. An example: I heard a small child crying her little heart out on a city bus recently. My initial response was a feeling of empathy for the crying child and for her mother who was trying to comfort her. Then the questions: What's going on? Can I help the mother? Should I reach out to the child? What would be *the* good? As I deliberated, several options presented themselves. I could offer support to the mother or to the child or I could decide, as in fact I did, to take no action.

What brought me to this decision? I am not sure what was going through my head at the moment of choice, but now as I think about it, an image appears of a child lost in a department store (the child is me) and wanting only to be found by someone who knew my name. This may have contributed to my judgment (of fact) that the mother could best meet the child's need, and my own eventual choice not to act, based on what I had come to know. The point I want to make here is that responsibility may begin with a feeling response to a situation but the final decision to choose the good of value includes the intelligent gathering of sufficient data and a judgment *this is a real good* that inspires the choice to act. In other words, the same human capacity of moving intelligently from experience to understanding to judgment of what is true or real is operative except that now the authentic person of good conscience apprehends and assents to the real as the *good*.

The fragility of human desire striving to create authentic selves out of the stuff of lived experience comes through dramatically in the essays written by students who have reflected on their own experience of deliberation and decision. One young man wrote about his decision to accompany his girl friend through an abortion. He described the circumstances of their lives – they were both students – and the significance to him of a woman's choice to have a child or not. It seemed to him at the time that they had good reasons to choose to terminate the pregnancy. Then, in the last paragraph of his essay, he wrote about his feelings at the recent baptism of his cousin's baby. He wondered why he had felt so sad and found himself weeping during the ceremony.

Programmed to be spectators in the flow of life, most of us are more attuned to what is expected of us by others than to the undercurrent of personal desire carrying us along to the freedom to be an authentic self making responsible decisions based on our own informed conscience. The habit of responsibility does not come automatically with age or genes or good example but from trial and error and the willingness to learn as we go.

Developmental psychologists Piaget, Erikson, Kohlberg and Kegan have done extensive research on moral consciousness (conscience) and human development. Their studies reveal that moral consciousness begins when the child moves beyond the boundaries of the undifferentiated world of *we* to a primitive consciousness of being an *I* in the face of the *other*. Because we are existentially *we* before we become *I*, our sense of self normally expands from a state of fusion with the external world to a state of personal autonomy and freedom of consciousness.[12] It may take years (or it may never happen) before the developing child moves beyond the dominant parental conscience toward the realization that in a concrete situation, since *I* am the one organizing the response here *I* am responsible for my choices.[13]

Several years ago, an American drug firm employed researchers to test various birth control methods on women in India, but chose *not* to include in the published data the fact that some women had experienced chronic bleeding from the use of the IUD coil. Later, the coil was successfully marketed without letting the women who would use it know what the researchers had learned about the possible side-effects. When questioned, the CEO defended the decision to keep the information hidden by saying that he was responsible to make money for the company. What motivated this decision? Fear, anxiety, rationalization, greed or just plain willfulness can deflect the initial intention to do *the good*.

A summer visit to the East Village in New York City gave one student the ambience to reflect on his own evolving understanding of consciousness becoming authentic conscience. He had lived alone for thirty days in a friend's apartment while attending an acting workshop. He compared himself with Jesus spending forty days in the desert. *He went away because he needed to see how much of him was him and how much was coming from other voices.* He described an insight that came one night while he was dancing (for eight hours!) in a club: *I saw who kept my walls up and I understood who I was and how I came to be. I understood that all my experiences were who I was and my future experiences will determine who I will become. I developed a passion for my own life.*

He explained how his new understanding of himself began to inform his conscience: I challenge my own opinions and measure growth (in knowledge) by seeing if my opinion has changed. If it hasn't changed, then I haven't learned anything new. Conscience is like a musical instrument. The more you practice on it the better you become acquainted with it. The less you tamper with it the easier it is to become clones – people who live in an accommodating bubble with their set of rules. Lonergan has them pegged as drifters. To experience friends with different values contributes to personal growth... The one thing I do have in common with everyone I meet is the struggle to be human. (Gabriel Lavina)

To struggle, as Gabriel did to become attentive, intelligent, reasonable and responsible, requires the vigilant willingness of an active learner consciously engaged in the search for *the* good. The burden of reflection is heavy and the human spirit can shut down or mute the sound of questions such as: *What's it worth? What can I do? What shall I do?* Lonergan reminds us:

> To achieve the good one has to know the real. To know the real, one has to reach the truth. To reach the truth one has to understand, to grasp the intelligible. To grasp the intelligible, one has to attend to the data. Each successive level of operations presupposes and complements its predecessors. The topmost level is the level of deliberate control and self control; there consciousness becomes conscience.[14]

In other words, consciousness becomes conscience when our knowing has become consistent with our living. What students seem to be most grateful for is how Lonergan's explanation of authentic conscience assumes human freedom to choose *the* good. Moral consciousness (authentic conscience) is not based on a set of imposed rules or moral principles but on the intentional decisions of the dynamically developing *free and responsible* human person *producing the first and only edition of himself.*[15]

the first and only edition of oneself....

Lonergan describes the kind of person who lives with a dependency on conceptual thinking or externally imposed principles or formulations of *the* good as a *truncated subject* who overlooks the concrete mode of human understanding and ignores the dynamic unity of human *being and becoming*. Ideally, the authentic human *being* emerges as a unity of active intelligence and feelings.[16] The lawyer who said in a radio interview, "as a lawyer, I would…but as a human being, I would…" in my view, is an example of a truncated subject who chooses to replace concrete, active human understanding with the concept of obligation.

The root meaning of the word obligation, 'to bind,' implies a rule or law imposed by another to which we *feel* bound. For instance, there is a law that obliges all who drive cars to learn how to drive, to be conscious and to be sober before sitting behind the wheel of a car. Most of us who drive cars have no problem accepting this kind of obligation. We feel responsible when we take the wheel of a car.

Obligation is a good because it makes trust and security possible in a shared world. It facilitates what philosophers name the good of order, the experience of order that civilization provides. Parents set this up for their children. Governments set this up for the population. Living together, we normally assume an infrastructure of rational norms and laws. When the imposed obligation is an obvious good and the authority imposing it is trustworthy, the obligation is usually accepted without question. No harm is done.

The *truncated subject's* response to external obligation has resulted in the greatest tragedies of recent human history. The trial of Adolph Eichmann gives the world an image of such a man. He simply failed to make the distinction between the self he was free to create and the self he accepted through obligation. Responsible for the transportation of human beings to the death camps, Eichmann accepted the value judgments of the people who assigned the work instead of making value judgments of his own.

The Political Philosopher Hannah Arendt says Eichmann was able to do this not because he had no conscience, but because his *conscience spoke with the respectable voice of respectable society around him*.[17] Eichmann saw himself as one of the insignificant cogs in his country's administrative wheel. The human spirit had shut down. The human capacity and freedom of consciousness to create himself through deliberation, evaluation and decision was inoperative and beyond his imagination. He felt no moral responsibility. The questions: *What is it worth? What can I do? What shall I do?* did not arise for him.

To read Arendt's account of Eichmann's trial is to discover a man who was docile, mindlessly obedient and externally defined. When asked by the trial judge to reflect on his preferences, Eichmann admitted that his choices were determined by his own desire for success. The only item on his scale of preference – his only chosen good (value) – was the self defined by others and what they expected of him. When asked to reflect on what had motivated his choices, he said that what he'd really wanted was to improve his bowling score and to secure a higher position on the administrative ladder. He seemed confused by the court's expectation that he should have recognized the consequences of his work. The only edition of the self he had created by his choices had muted the feelings that would have expanded his horizon and perhaps altered his judgment of values.[18]

Just as the detached disinterested desire to know is a feeling that moves us beyond the desire for certainty to judge what is true, so the desire for the good is a feeling that moves us to transcend mere self-satisfaction to use our human intelligence and power to deliberate and evaluate before choosing what we have judged to be genuinely worthwhile or valuable or good. Feelings, says Lonergan, channel our attention, shape our horizon and give direction to our lives. *Without feelings our knowing and deciding would be paper thin.* Feelings are what give intentional consciousness *its mass, momentum drive, power.*[19] We create consistency between our knowing and our living by marshalling all our human resources. And yet, in the process of *producing the first and only edition of himself...*the *free and responsible existential subject...*may come to understand...*he makes himself good or evil.*[20]

he makes himself evil...

The human capacity to choose *the* good by deliberation, evaluation and human choice is easier to accept than to ask if we are actually responsible for unleashing evil energy in the world. But how do we explain the effects of evil choices? The question makes us squirm. Evil seems so random, out of our control, inflicted rather than deliberately caused or chosen. It just happens!

A video clip of the life of physicist Richard Feynman provides students with an image to unpack with questions about the presence of evil in our world. Asked about his participation in the Los Alamos project to build the atomic bomb, Feynman says that he came to understand that what he did was morally wrong, but he didn't think much about right or wrong while he was working on the project. It didn't occur to him until much later that he was responsible for the consequences of his choice. He joined in the parties and played his bongo drum and drank beer with the others as they celebrated the project's success. Feynman's emphatic statement: *I didn't let myself think* provides the clue that guides the learning process from experience to intelligent questions. What is evil? Where does it come from? What can we do about it?[21]

We need tools to help us get a hold on human evil as we experience it in our own lives. Tools that will help us to face the consequences and not simply look for escape. Most students haven't given *evil* much thought and are grateful for the opportunity to reflect together with others who share their questions. Our intention is not to find a rational solution, but to understand how humans usually respond to what is perceived as evil and what we can do in the face of the experience. Whether evil is the result of intentional human choices – our own or others – the psychic chaos it creates in us is felt as an inner assault and the response is the same whether we perceive the assault as deliberate or not. How do we respond to evil?

We ask *why?* We close our eyes, hide our face, turn away and try to escape. We seek the presence of other people, a shelter where we can huddle and hide to share the experience. Instinctively we know there is no sense to be found here. Parents who have lost a child through the carelessness of a drunk driver feel it as another blow when *reasons* are offered as consolation. I am thinking of a neighbor who had just come home from the hospital after his five-year-old son, originally thought to have the flu, had died suddenly of meningitis. When I walked into his house, he screamed at me from the depths of his loss: *Don't tell me God wanted him in heaven!* This, I learned later, were the words of comfort his equally distraught mother had offered. As a matter of fact, I was at a loss to find any words to carry meaning. Instinctively, all I wanted was to be with them to support them in their pain. I knew that explanations would be no support at all. There is nothing in such a senseless loss for intelligence to grasp.

Lonergan reflects on the human tendency to escape the consequences of evil choices. *The first and most common escape is to*

avoid self-consciousness...the second escape is rationalization... the third is
giving up hope of amending its ways.[22]

There is a scene in the film The Boys of St. Vincent that portrays this three-fold response to the fact of evil better than anything I could imagine or express. Brother Lavin has been accused, but never convicted, of pedophilia in a Newfoundland orphanage. He eventually leaves religious life, marries and fathers two children. When he receives notice that criminal charges have been laid and he will soon be brought to trial, an agonizing scene follows with his wife who loves him and asks for the truth; he denies any wrongdoing. There is a frightening scene with the court psychiatrist whom Lavin cons into believing his story. There is a scene where he's alone – his armor beginning to crumble – where we see a glimmer of hope that reality may be grasped. Instead, what we're given is an image of human evil in all its complexity. Lavin's face suddenly contorts as he slams the table to banish from his life what he does not want to be – and what he will not allow to be. When he slams the table a second time, the viewer understands that Lavin has chosen to shut out of consciousness the evil he has done. And with this choice to deny reality, he shuts out any hope that good may be restored in his life.[23]

Are free human beings responsible for evil? Lonergan says that human evil – or what he names *basic sin* – is the result of the *contraction of consciousness*. By ignoring questions that arise, effectively, the human spirit shrinks and loses its capacity to go beyond the concrete experience to ask the questions for understanding. The deliberate choice not to ask (to deny) the questions: *What is true? What is good?* provides the escape route from the consequences of understanding for oneself and begins the spiraling process that leads to rationalization and hopelessness. To the extent that evil in the world is the result of human unwillingness to deliberate, evaluate and make decisions based on judgments of the true and the good, evil is an intentional human choice for which we humans are responsible.[24]

In the last two chapters of *Insight*, Lonergan directly addresses the problem of evil where he announces bluntly that since evil is a problem, there must be a rational solution, and the explanation may be found in the ultimate intelligibility of that which he calls *God*. Yet, for most of us, this explanation found even in the mind of God doesn't tell us how to live with the consequences of evil choices because:

> *...explanation does not give man a home...one has to admit ...that man's explanatory self-knowledge can become effective in his concrete living only if the content of systematic insights, the direction of judgments, the dynamism of decision can be embodied in images that release feeling and emotion and flow spontaneously into deeds no less than words.*[25]

In other words, he is suggesting that the home we seek may be found embodied in images more than words. *Images that release feeling and emotion* (symbols) cannot promise a rational solution to the problem of evil but since they *flow spontaneously into deeds...* they offer shelter from the chaos. Symbols make sensible what human intelligence reaches for and give us a way to face the irrationality of evil head on. Symbols provide the psychic energy we need to accept the reality and move on. Lonergan says: *Inasmuch as intelligence and reasonableness and willingness issue into human words matched with deeds, they need at their disposal images so charged with affects (i.e. symbols) that they succeed both in guiding and in propelling action.*[26]

If we accept this explanation that the spiraling towards evil begins with the human choice to refuse questions for understanding, *contraction of consciousness*, can we also accept Lonergan's suggestion that symbols provide a way to live with the consequences? Can symbols transform human consciousness, provide shelter from the assault of evil and offer a way of hope that goodness will prevail?[27]

The answer to our desperate *why? why? why?* in response to evil is not found in rational explanations after all, but in the deed – one man squeezing the hand of another – that becomes a symbol of transforming goodness. The psychic energy of symbol propels human living towards hope and the possibility of *the* good.

Finally....

Years ago, I taught catechism once a week after school to a group of sixth-grade Mexican-American children in a small town in Arizona. I noticed that one of my students had missed class for a couple of weeks and phoned her home. Her mother told me that Gloria had leukemia and was in the hospital in Phoenix. She was not expected to live long. Then came this desperate plea: *Could you tell her something about death? Her father and I are so angry we can't talk to her about dying. I don't know what to say.*

A few days later, in a state of heightened anxiety, I drove the two hundred and fifty miles to Phoenix. Feeling the assault of a child's meaningless suffering as something evil, I wondered what words of mine could possibly help a ten-year-old accept death. The hand that also held the steering wheel of the car gripped a small crucifix. When I arrived at the hospital, Gloria's little body was already turning blue from internal bleeding but she was conscious and glad to see me. Her mother thanked me for coming and left the room.

Gloria, do you know what's happening to you?

Yes, they said I will die, but I don't know what will happen then.

I don't know either – nobody knows exactly

I remembered the crucifix still in my hand, and held it so she could grasp it as well. I said something like: Jesus died too. He said he would be there for us when we die. I don't know what it will be like, but I imagine it will be like going through a dark tunnel and coming into the light at the end and meeting Jesus there.

I left the room, hugged the mother and cried with her. I drove home numb.

A few days later I received a phone call to tell me Gloria had died. Her mother reported that in the last few minutes of her life here, Gloria looked at her and said, *Don't worry, Mommy, he's there.* At that moment, the bitterness she and her husband had felt during their daughter's illness had vanished. Gloria's final gift was hope.

Experience of grace…is experience of man's capacity for self-transcendence, of his unrestricted openness to the intelligible, the true, the good.

It is experience of a twofold frustration of that capacity: the objective frustration of life in a world distorted by sin; the subjective frustration of one's incapacity to break with one's own evil ways.

It is experience of a transformation one did not bring about but rather underwent…as it let one's circumstances shift, one's dispositions change, new encounters occur, and – so gently and quietly – one's heart be touched.

Bernard Lonergan, Mission and the Spirit

According to St. Thomas, divine life is not laid over the surface of our understanding like an external additive; rather it is infused at the root of our being.

Divine life is built up in us according to the framework of our nature, even as it surpasses our nature ontologically.

We can say that grace is within us after the fashion of a (super) nature; that is to say, after the fashion of a principle most interior to ourselves, most our own, at the same time that it is divine.

It is the dynamic force of grace that makes us capable of living communion with God.

Marie-Dominique Chenu, O.P., Aquinas and his role in Theology

6. Creativity and Self-transcendence – where do we go from here?

Most university students today are not helped by the system of beliefs and values that support their parents' search for meaning. Instead, they construct their own meaning hesitantly around personal experience and testing. For some, this involves experimentation with drugs and sexuality. Since more than half of them belong to divorced families, they have learned to expect and live with impermanence. They survive the world of rapid change by keeping their options open and making few commitments. They either accept the culture of their peers uncritically or filter inherited values through the authority of their own life experience. Educators no longer expect students to believe what they say simply because an authority figure says it is so.

Some students grow weary of the effort to create meaning for themselves and run for cover under the false security of fundamentalism. False, because they hand over to someone else the natural right to engage their own intelligence and critical judgment in the learning process. Both the drifter and the person who stops asking questions shut down the unique capacity of the human spirit for self-transcendence and for hope that human meaning can be achieved.

It is unrealistic for me to assume that students in the Creative Self course will accept, as I do, Lonergan's claim that the goal of self-transcendence is fulfilled in the mystical union of being in love with *that which is called God*. The course draws students from a variety of religious traditions, and from no religious tradition. While many find Lonergan's religious language and symbol system useful in creating meaning, most students that I meet do not. Some even resist his use of the word 'God.'

Still, as a teacher I continue to search for the word or sign or gesture that will engage them in the *question* of what it is we continue to reach for after we have come to knowledge. The fact that most of them are willing to risk the surprise of discovery keeps me searching for ways to keep alive the question they usually ask themselves at the end of the course: *where do we go from here?* They know by now I don't expect them to accept Lonergan's answers – or mine – but when they hear him ask this question: *Is the universe on our side, or are we just gamblers, perhaps fools?* his words resonate with their experience.[1]

In the time between the writing of *Insight* and *Method* Lonergan seems to have discovered that place in human consciousness where intelligence and feeling converge. In *Insight*, readers were invited to identify and claim the workings of their own minds. In *Method*, Lonergan has moved beyond the realm of faculty psychology and invites readers to become aware of their own experience as existential subjects *being* consciously attentive, intelligent, reasonable, responsible. Feelings have become part of the story of the unique human capacity for self-transcendence. *Detached, disinterested desire* has expanded from knowing to loving. In his later work, Lonergan says that the unrestricted desire for knowledge meets the insatiable longing for love in the deepest core of the human spirit: the feelings of the human heart. *Just as unrestricted questioning is our capacity for self-transcendence, so, being in love in an unrestricted fashion is the proper fulfillment of that capacity.*[2]

We all have moments when we have become a *be-ing in love*. Ask any young couple how the birth of their first child has altered their lives and transformed their understanding of what it means to be human. When they find themselves foregoing mere satisfaction to love unconditionally this new person needing twenty-four hour care, the human capacity for self-transcendence is no longer a lofty philosophical ideal. It becomes for them an existential experience that is also transforming. As I stood with my niece Susan admiring her new daughter, she said: *I didn't know our hearts could expand so!*

Yielding to the momentum of the 13 week course, most students are aware that they have become more conscious of themselves attending to data, questioning intelligently, making critical judgments based on available evidence and deliberating, evaluating and making responsible decisions of value. In other words, they recognize themselves learning to become creative selves by *living* consciously Lonergan's precepts: be attentive, be intelligent, be reasonable, be responsible.

Having claimed the capacity for intelligent inquiry and critical appropriation of their own learning power, they also recognize the transformation of their way of being existentially in their world. This excerpt from Barbara's final essay says it well:

Over the past few months, I have learned the great importance of paying attention, of questioning, of reflecting, judging and seeking the truth, and of deciding and applying what I've come to know, of choosing goodness. My awareness of myself has changed. I am now on the road to self-transcendence. Everyday I work at developing the freedom to follow eros, and this is something I will carry with me long after I leave the classroom.

When students ask, toward the end of the course: *where do we go from here?* I wonder how Lonergan, the teacher, would respond to their question. This imaginary dialogue between the philosopher-theologian and students in the course is part of the wondering.

Natalie: *I have definitely come a long way. I had written the first assignment (describe an experience that evoked in you real questions) about two friends who had passed away due to a drug overdose. After these losses I found myself searching for some kind of answer to why it happened. I am not a practicing Catholic and neither am I an atheist, but I am open to adopt a concept that will aid me in my journey to understanding. The class discussion of the word "longing" added to my awareness and comprehension.*

I had been denying the fact that there is an underlying mysterious truth that resides in the epitome of our being. I had been struggling with the fact that this feeling was real. I believe that the course has made me more open and less skeptical of the possibilities of human beings. I also believe that I knew this to a certain extent before, yet I thought only those who held religious beliefs were entitled to speak of it. Now I feel liberated, not because

I have the answers but because I can trust my faith in the world again and be a part of the bigger picture that is beyond us all.

Lonergan: I congratulate you for following through on your own questions about death and what it means for human life. Because you choose to face the *bigger picture* filtering through your own consciousness, you are already on a trajectory toward the source of that *mysterious truth that resides in the epitome of our being.* The courage to ask the question *why* is your tentative nod toward the ultimate source of intelligibility or *that which is called God.*

Another student who exhibited her willingness to learn by coming to every class, asking lots of questions and doing all the assigned work said that she had learned something valuable from Lonergan, *even though he was a Jesuit!* She appreciated the fact that he expected her to understand how her mind works and then to use it to ask her own questions. However, she didn't accept Lonergan's belief that the human capacity to come to truth was somehow a share in the wisdom of that which is called 'God.'

Jessica: *What about non-believers like me?*

Lonergan: Intelligent inquiry opens us to *all* there is to understand and so leads to the not unreasonable hope that the *all* that draws the human heart and intelligence includes *that which is called God.* The choice to shut down the spontaneous flow of questions that might lead us to the question of God would be unreasonable. This excludes even the possibility of ultimate intelligibility. When the question of God arises, we have already been moved by that which is called 'God.' I've said many times that the refusal of the next question – any question – is the primary cause of despair and decline in human history. The *flight from understanding* is a *disease* ravaging our own times. To dismiss the question of God results in a *shrinking of human consciousness.* This refusal, I believe, is a sin against life. The more important question than the one about God's existence is the one that arises with the stirring of the human heart to love and says: *how shall I respond?* In other words, I believe that the question of God *arises* as a question *because* we have first been touched by *that which is called God.*[3]

I have conceived being in love with God an ultimate fulfillment of man's capacity for self-transcendence; and this view of religion is sustained when God is conceived as the supreme fulfillment of the transcendental notions, as supreme intelligence, truth, reality, righteousness, goodness.[4]

Jessica: *I have always stopped at the mention of God because it seems like that takes away something of our responsibility to ourselves and replaces it by putting the onus on God to shape the kind of person I am becoming. What I understand now is that which we call 'God' contributes to our creative selves, and that isn't necessarily a bad thing.*

Lonergan: Yes, if you believe that the creation initiated by 'God' continues in you as you create the person you are becoming, responsibility is not diminished, rather empowered by participation in the Whole on going creative act. Your freedom remains intact.

Sarah: *Creativity isn't just an abstract notion – it refers to a positive course of action requiring a consciously engaged self to take risks and follow through on those risks: to question and appropriate; to be responsible and true. Our inherent creativity will begin to manifest itself in every aspect of our lives...It is by no means a linear process, nor should it ever end. Best ride of your life!*

Lonergan: I notice by your headscarf that you are a Muslim. Let me make clear my belief that regardless of one's religious orientation, those of us who yield as you do to the undertow of our lives as a question have become engaged in the existential experience of Mystery, call it what you will. By surrendering to the dynamism of intelligent inquiry in the scope of our experiencing – in the insight of our understanding – in the truth of our judgment – in the goodness of our choices – we move into the limitless horizon that I like to think of as the *known Unknown or the Mystery*. Then our creative learning and living incarnates the existential question: *How shall I respond to this kindling of the heart drawing me into the greater mystery.*

A former student now studying journalism, had just returned from six months in India traveling and learning meditation and yoga when we met, on the run, in the library. Reisa belongs to the Jewish tradition.

Was India wonderful? I asked.

Yes. I thought of you often and how the course had prepared me for what I needed to learn there.

How?

It helped me understand that I am part of the process.

Lonergan: If you have come to understand yourself as part of a process, you have already accepted life as a gift. I am reminded of Dag Hammarskjöld, former secretary general of the United Nations, who wrote of a day in his own life when he was able to say: *For All that has been Thanks, for all that shall be, Yes.* I call this the experience of grace...*the experience of a transformation one did not bring about but rather underwent...as it let one's circumstances shift, one's dispositions change, new encounters occur, and – so gently and quietly – one's heart be touched.*[5]

Nina: *Like many people of my generation I didn't grow up in a very religious environment and by my teenage years, I had pretty much abandoned all connection to religion. Still, something within drove me to wonder about the ultimate purpose of existence, and I knew that this was something that I had to discover for myself. Gradually, I established a connection to 'the mystery' based on the unfolding and opening of my own self.* (Nina writes of an experience from the previous summer, while meditating under a tree, that left her with a strong conviction of being connected to the universe) *I don't think that you can necessarily precipitate this kind of experience by saying 'okay I'm open' and I don't think that the experience itself is the entire point either. What such experiences do, it seems, is encourage a sense of reverence for all life, a recognition that at the core we are all one, that we can put in practice in everyday life, in our interactions with each other and with the world.*

Lonergan: This kind of *recognition* that you speak of comes at different stages of our life as we come to understand in a new way that *the experience of the mystery of love and awe is not objectified. It remains within subjectivity as a vector, an undertow, a fateful call to dreaded holiness.*[6]

When I was sixty years old, this call echoed through every tissue of my own life. In the summer of 1964, I came back from Rome to

Toronto excited about an insight I had had about theological method that I felt would pull together the pieces of a book I was writing on *Method in Theology*. This book had been in my mind for more than thirty years – even before *Insight*. During a regular medical check-up that summer I was thrown into the Mystery in a big way when I was diagnosed with lung cancer. The series of operations that followed in the next year left me weak and vulnerable, and even close to death at times. I thought the book would never be realized. But, I did get better and as I look back now I realize that this health crisis had given me a new experience and understanding of what it meant to be loved by God. I was cared for, unconditionally, by people who convinced me that I was lovable. I came to understand – in the fiber of my own being – these words from Scripture that I could now repeat with conviction: *The love of God has been poured forth in our hearts by the Holy Spirit which has been given to us. (Romans 5:5)*

Lonergan's articulation of the transforming effect of being in love was there in his earlier work, but in *Method*, and later his writing shimmers with this deeper experience of love gratuitously given and received.[7]

Nina: *I related to* what you said about: *becoming oneself …is…a becoming aware, a growth in self-consciousness, a heightening of one's self appropriation, that is possible because our separate unrevealed hidden cores have a common circle of reference, the human community, and an ultimate point of reference, which is God who is all in all.*[8]

Lonergan: When I gave this talk to my fellow Jesuits I intended to give it the title: *On Being Oneself.* I am glad you got the point that when you strive to become authentically who you are, you give the best possible gift to 'God.' I don't think it is unreasonable to hope that human achievements – even our own – can have ultimate significance. *Faith and progress have a common root in (man's) cognitional and moral self-transcendence. To promote either is to promote the other indirectly. Faith places human efforts in a friendly universe; it reveals an ultimate significance in human achievement; it strengthens new undertakings with confidence.*[9]

Natalie: the class discussion of the word 'longing' brought me back to the lithography I had made in another class. The first piece I created was entitled 'Longing.' There is an obvious change in someone when they experience a meaningful occurrence and gain insight from it as well. There is a definite longing to express what they have come to know. I realize now that when we become conscious of the ache longing creates within we can either drift or ask...what can I hope for?

In 1975, when Lonergan spoke about the *emerging religious consciousness of our time* reflecting the transition from *lesser to greater luminousness, intensity, clarity, fullness,* he reflects a shift in his understanding of how *grace* functions in contemporary religious experience.[10] The traditional metaphysical language that explains grace as something superimposed on human nature has disappeared and he speaks of *grace achieved* when humans respond to God's self-communication. I wonder if this shift in his thinking includes the understanding that the locus of God's self communication extends the realm of religious experience to the experience of self-transcendence now accessible in all creative living. When Lonergan says that *religion* draws attention to *the prior word God speaks to us by flooding our hearts with his love...the experience of the mystery of love and awe,* he seems to be saying that it is in the *experience of the mystery of love and awe* that 'God' meets the human heart and the experience precedes any attempt to exhaustively explain it in religious language.[11]

In the open space of no religious boundaries, students in the creative self course often describe their own yielding to self transcendence as the longed for *more* that breaks into their own lives and clarifies just what it means to be human. A dance student explained her acceptance of an unplanned pregnancy and the responsibility of being a single mother: *I realized that something greater than myself was at work in me.* Others surprised themselves by being able to stay up all night with a sick friend, or sharing (with hardship) their living quarters and food, being present to someone overcoming addictions, or someone suffering personal loss in a failed relationship, all the while feeling their heart's capacity expanding.

The point I would make here is that when these young people reflect on their experience of mystery as love and awe, and when they speak about their own *experience of a transformation one did not bring about but rather underwent,* I recognize the idiom of the divine speaking of what it means to be human in our times.

A conversation I once had with my nephew David comes to mind. He was performing the role of Marius in the Canadian production of *Les Miserables* in Toronto. The day after I had attended the performance, we were having breakfast with other members of the cast and I, as usual struggling for words, wanted to tell them how grateful I was for the gift of their performance. *It was an experience of transcendence for me,* I said. They looked puzzled and then, a woman who had so brought me out of myself into the mystery the night before replied: *transcendence...what a wonderful word...what does it mean?* It dawned on me then that they could *do* transcendence – going beyond their own skins in nine grueling performances a week – and share that experience with me as well, without having the language to express what was happening.

Finally...

Consciously engaged in the dynamism of their own learning and living, spiraling from experience to understanding to critical assent to responsible life choices, students find themselves identifying the transcendent capacity of the human spirit moving toward fulfillment in their own lives. Claire, a creative writing student, says it well:

I don't have a mountain to climb, a skill to develop, so much as a person to BE. This course helped me realize that it isn't silly and weak-willed and stupidly idealistic when I think of how that autistic boy grabbed my hands and spoke to me in his own words, how he just looked at me and did that, and I realized that the moment gave me more, infinitely more, than any technically polished poem I'd written could ever truly be praised... I'd always say 'I am this way (learning disabled) to help people who have felt stupid feel less stupid.' This voice and idea never went away. After this semester I'm starting to realize what I always wanted to see as true: that whatever I do fully (not always writing) is me realizing my potential. That my skill isn't words on a page but a heart and a drive and an insight that can be manifested in more than one way... I like to keep my heart open and know it's strong.

All this to say that students can recognize the deepest longings of their hearts moving toward the *Mystery*. When they accept as their own the human capacity for self-transcendence, creative learners flourish in a *friendly universe* where they are free to breathe and *be* and to leave a trace of creative living in the world.

The artist establishes his insights
not by proof or verification,
but by skillfully embodying them in colors and shapes,
in sounds and movements,
in the unfolding situations and actions of fiction.
To the spontaneous joy of conscious living
is added the spontaneous joy of free intellectual creation.

Bernard Lonergan, Insight

Conclusion

In the late sixties, Time magazine described Bernard Lonergan as *not an easy thinker to appreciate* but one who deserved attention because as a thinker who was also a teacher he recognized the necessity of addressing those issues that were influencing what was going forward in educational practice.

Values, once embedded in the very structure of the university, are in danger of being lost. The human element, which I have claimed to be the natural right of students to grow and to learn, has been submerged by other more pressing concerns to keep the system going. Teachers, once honored with the sacred trust of teaching others to discover for themselves how to live the good life, wonder what they have to contribute to student learning in our day. Students play the game and gain credentials without ever engaging their own minds or experiencing the joy of learning for themselves. Since most of them accept the educational system as given, they also live without hope of leaving a trace of themselves in the world.

Finally...

If the human exchange between teachers and students were restored to the teaching-learning process, and the educational system of our day embraced as an ideal the discovery of oneself as a free and intelligent person consciously engaged in creative learning and living, what *good* would it *do?*

Students would use their own minds....

As they identify and claim the workings of their own mind, students would become aware that abstract ideas about meaning, truth and values actually emerge from the conscious experience of ordinary human questions – their own. *The effort to live is fundamentally the struggle for meaning...spiraling upwards...willing to accept the creative opportunity....*[1] Peter explains how he accepted the creative opportunity that life offered him:

I wanted to understand why a personal relationship had gone wrong. I started to ask some questions of my experience and it started to make some sense. Whereas when I was going through it, it didn't make any sense at all. It was a big risk – to try to learn something from experience. It wasn't simply an academic exercise. It takes a lot of courage to ask the real questions that come to us when we open ourselves to experience.

Paul was a student in the political science program. He said that his academic advisor had asked him: *Why are you taking this creative self course? It sounds so Californian!* He didn't have a quick answer to the question, but later he thought that for the first time in three years of university schooling he was actually using his own mind and articulating his own thoughts. As he left the building one day, he said he surprised himself by continuing to think about the questions we had just explored in class.

Following through on the questions that beat at the walls of consciousness dissolves the kind of hopelessness expressed by the question: *who the hell cares?* Lonergan's theory of how we come to understand and know provides students with a method of creative learning and living that gives structure to the universal human desire to make sense of one's own life experience. He also offers them a philosophical home, an anchor in the *pulsing flow of life,* and hope as they struggle to make meaning and to connect with something bigger than themselves.

Debbie, a former student, during a chance meeting in a Montreal café, tells me she has switched her university program because as she explains: *I know what I want to learn now.* I listen in awe, because I know that her choice of two additional years of study will mean two more years of waiting on tables. What comes back to me in a flash is the response paper she wrote a year ago when she explained how she *got it!* Debbie had been feeling *dumb* as she sat on the bus reading for the third time the week's assignment. All of a sudden she began laughing uncontrollably, because she understood for herself what Lonergan meant by the self-appropriation of the knower. She realized, *it's me he's talking about – he's telling me to use my own intelligence!* And she had just done it – used her own mind to grasp the point he was making when he wrote: *The ideal of knowledge is myself as intelligent, as asking intelligent questions, as requiring intelligible answers.*[2]

The truth that makes us free for creative learning and living is not found out there in someone else's thought but in the dynamism of one's own human spirit being attentive, intelligent, critically reasonable and responsible. Students who have become conscious of what they were doing as they grasped the intelligible pattern in accumulated data (insight) and critically apprehended and assented to the evidence gathered (judgment) and deliberated, and evaluated and come to responsible decisions about what is worthwhile, have actualized their own capacity to know the real. This doesn't mean that following through on the spiraling desire of the human spirit to know will lead to changeless certainty. The *Mystery* that draws us also stretches the capacity for human understanding and makes it a shrine for holiness.

For years after publishing *Insight*, Lonergan continued to pursue the question of understanding the operations of the human mind and what it is we do when we come to know. He invited his readers to participate in the on-going question by attending to the operations of their own minds:

Initially, the human mind is just a black box: the input we know is sensation, the output we know is talk. But what precisely goes on in between to transform the input into the output? Down the millennia consensus has not been obtained.[3]

Students would engage in dialogue with others....

Lonergan's explanation of what we do when we come to know offers us a beacon of hope that we can learn to live with people with different values and meaning systems. When students have claimed the workings of their own minds, they expect others to operate with that same innate human capacity for intelligent inquiry, rational judgment and responsible living. They become more secure in their own traditions and less defensive when meeting other traditions of learning and living. By acquiring the tools to live creatively within the fragmented sensibility of a pluralistic world, students become willing to listen and learn from others without needing to argue for their own position. When students were asked to name one thing they would take away from the course, a strictly observant orthodox Jewish woman said it was what she had learned from an Islamic man in the class...*how he thought about things*. She had never before had a conversation with a Muslim.

Students who have claimed the capacity of their own minds hope to find a common ground where they can work together to make something *good* of the world they share. Each person's creative response to the *pulsing flow of life* is valued within a collaborative dialogue of mutual understanding when the ideal of education has become student learning. Because students have experienced themselves as learners, they are free to learn from all that life offers. Keith says it well:

I have on the wall above my computer the word 'vicarious' it means experiencing through somebody else's experience. Lonergan says we must not experience things vicariously, but must pay attention as we experience things for ourselves. This, to me, is an incredibly freeing thing. Once you experience yourself understanding, then you are free to learn other things.

When educators accept the task of contributing to the *re-creation of* students' *freedom of consciousness*, the human exchange between teacher and student will be restored to the learning process. Lonergan has said that creative learning and living is nothing mysterious. *The artistic moment simply breaks away from ordinary living and is, as it were, an opening, a moment of new potentiality.*[4]

When educators have found creative ways to engage this current generation of students in their own learning, they will also keep humanity as a whole from going off the rails. Or so I like to believe.

Students will learn to dance the Flamenco...

One last dramatic image to unpack will deepen our understanding of the human element in the teaching-learning process. A short film documents a Flamenco lesson at the National Ballet School of Canada taught by two teachers from Spain. The dominant image of Flamenco keeps alive Lonergan's notion that engaged learning transforms the *being* of the learner. It also helps students to understand for themselves the meaning of terms they have already heard: *self appropriation – self transcendence – engaged intelligence.*

After the initial surprise that a film about Flamenco dancing teaches us about learning, students have no difficulty recognizing how the teachers – Antonio and Susanna – efficiently convey the elements of the dance, but expect the ballet students to do their own internal work in the process. Rhythm, steps and movement are external tools absorbed into the muscular memory of the body.

Lonergan's notion of self-appropriation ceases to be a mere term when the ballet students finally step into the center of the circle to demonstrate what they have learned. It is clear which ones have made the content of the lesson their own. Some students have learned to repeat what the teachers have done – they have acquired external tools and a technique. Others, surrendering to the rhythm and movement from within, transcend the mere externals by unleashing a passionate burst of energy that *is* Flamenco. Braving to dance alone, they have left a trace of their presence in the world because they have grasped the inner meaning of both the dance and of Susanna's words: *To dance alone with courage is to face death...that is Flamenco!*

Notes

Introduction

1. Lonergan, Bernard. (1992) CW 3. *Insight: A Study of Human Understanding* edited by Frederick E. Crowe and Robert M. Doran. Toronto: University of Toronto Press.
2. Lorde, Audre. (1984) *Sister Outsider.* Freedom, California: Crossing Press, p. 79.
3. Lonergan, Bernard. (1993) CW 10. *Topics in Education.* Edited by Robert M. Doran and Frederick E. Crowe. Toronto: University of Toronto Press. p. 51.
4. Lonergan, Bernard. (1993) *Topics in Education.* p. 232.
5. Lonergan, Bernard. (1985) *A Third Collection.* Edited by Frederick Crowe. New York: Paulist Press, p. 175.
6. Lonergan, Bernard. (1997) CW 2. *Verbum: Word and Idea in Aquinas.* Toronto: University of Toronto Press. p. 85.
7. Lonergan, Bernard. (1972) *Method in Theology.* New York: Paulist Press. p. 103, 117.

Chapter 1. *What do we do when we teach?*

1. Lonergan, Bernard. (1992) *Insight: A Study in Human Understanding.* (CW 3) Toronto: University of Toronto Press. p. 210.
2. Doran, Robert. (1999) *System and History. The Challenge to Catholic Systematic Theology* Theological Studies Vol. 60. p. 652.
3. Lonergan, Bernard. (1985) *A Third Collection: Papers by Bernard J.F. Lonergan. S.J.* edited by Frederick E. Crowe. New York: Paulist Press. p. 103.
4. Lonergan, Bernard. (1988) *Collection. CW 4.* edited by Frederick Crowe and Robert Doran. Toronto: University of Toronto Press. p. 138.
5. Lonergan, Bernard. *Insight.* p. 197-198.
6. Gregson, Vernon. Editor (1989) *The Desires of the Human Heart.* New York: Paulist Press. p. 8.
7. Lonergan, Bernard. *Insight.* p. 199.
8. Scheffler, Israel. (1973) *Reason and Teaching.* "Philosophical Models of Teaching" Indianapolis and New York: Bobbs Merrill. p. 67.
9. Lonergan, Bernard. *Insight.* p. 28.
10. Lonergan, Bernard. *Insight.* p. 200.
11. Havel, Vaclav. (1989) *Letters to Olga.* New York: Henry Holt and Company. p. 347-355.
12. All excerpts from students' writing is used with their permission.
13. Lonergan, Bernard. (1993) *Topics in Education. (CW 10)* Toronto: University of Toronto Press. p. 199.
14. *Topics.* p. 211
15. *Topics.* p. 221.
16. *Topics.* p. 217.

Chapter 2. *Insight – we can all do it.*

1. Lonergan, Bernard. (1985) *A Third Collection: Papers by Bernard J.F. Lonergan, S.J.* edited by Frederick E. Crowe, S.J. New York: Paulist Press. p. 103.
2. Lonergan, Bernard. (1992) *Insight: A Study of Human Understanding.(CW3)* Toronto: University of Toronto Press. p. 28.
3. Ibid., p. 29. Lonergan told the story of one of his own students at the end of his course at the Thomas More Institute on *Thought and Reality (1945-46)* whacking his desk and saying "I've got it!" He said this gave him the reassurance he needed that he had the makings of a book on insight.
4. Lonergan, Bernard. (1992) *Insight.* p. 34.
5. Ibid., p. 29.
6. Scheffler, Israel. (1991) *In Praise of Cognitive Emotions.* New York: Routledge, p. 15.
7. Lonergan, Bernard. (1992) *Insight.* p. 29.
8. Ibid., p. 30. When I was studying Statistics for the first time, I asked why a certain principle always applied in like-situations. The professor, stood back and smiled and said: "That's a question for the music of the spheres – why? is a non-question here." He didn't understand my need to understand so that I could apply the principle with my own intelligence.
9. Lonergan, Bernard. (1993) *Topics in Education. (CW 10)* Toronto: University of Toronto Press. p. 209.
10. Keller, Helen. (1965) *The Story of My Life.* New York: Airmont Publishing, p. 272.
11. Ibid., p. 21
12. Lonergan, Bernard. (1992) *Insight.* p. 30.
13. Lonergan, Bernard. (1997) *Verbum: Word and Idea in Aquinas.* (CW 2) Toronto: University of Toronto Press. p. 193.

Chapter 3. *Imagination – hinders or helps creative learning and living*

1. Lonergan, Bernard. (1992) *Insight: A Study of Human Understanding (CW 3)* Toronto: University of Toronto Press. p. 212,
2. O'Connor, Flannery. (1987) *The Complete Stories.* New York: Farrar, Straus and Giroux, p. 405-420.
3. "Our Machines, Ourselves" an account of a forum published in Harper's Magazine, May 1997.
4. Hughes, Ted. (1994) *Winter Pollen: Occasional Prose.* Edited by William Scammell. "Myth and Education" London, Boston: Faber and Faber. p. 136-152.
5. Ibid., p. 151.
6. Bohm, David. (1998) *On Creativity.* Edited by Lee Nichol. London and New York: Routledge, p. 42.
7. Ibid., p. 53.
8. John Miller of the English Department at Concordia University generously contributed the gift of his expertise on Coleridge to my task. Miller disagrees with Bohm's interpretation of Coleridge on two major points: his use of a continuum (poles) rather than degrees to describe the primary and secondary imagination and his claim that Coleridge included "fancy" in the secondary imagination. Coleridge dismisses "fancy" as the mechanical power of the mind that simply shuffles and rearranges items of perception.
9. Coleridge, Samuel Taylor. *Biographia Literaria. Chapter 13.* p. 1588.
10. Barth, J. Robert. S.J. (1977) *The Symbolic Imagination: Coleridge and the Romantic Tradition.* New Jersey: Princeton University Press. p. 79-127.
11. Lonergan, Bernard. (1972) *Method in Theology.* New York: Paulist Press. p. 103.

12. Lonergan, Bernard. (1988) *Collection (CW 4)*. Edited by Frederick E. Crowe and Robert M. Doran. Toronto: University of Toronto Press. p. 138.
13. Lonergan, Bernard. (1997) *Verbum: Word and Idea in Aquinas. (CW 2)* Edited by Frederick E. Crowe and Robert M. Doran. Toronto: University of Toronto Press. p. 182-186.
14. Barth, p. 78.
15. Lonergan, Bernard. (1992) *Insight*. p. 214.
16. Lonergan, Bernard. (1985) *A Third Collection: Papers by Bernard J.F. Lonergan, S.J.*, edited by Frederick E. Crowe, S.J. New York: Paulist Press, p. 100-109.
17. Lonergan, Bernard. (1992) *Insight*, p. 196-269.
18. Ibid., p. 247.
19. Lonergan, Bernard. (1990) *Understanding and Being. (CW 5)* Edited by Elizabeth A. Morelli and Mark D. Morelli. Toronto: University of Toronto Press. p. 14.
20. Langer, Susanne K. (1957) *Philosophy in a New Key.* Cambridge, MA. Harvard University Press. p. 72.
21. Visser, Margaret. (2002) *Beyond Fate.* Toronto: Anansi Press. p. 57.
22. Kearney, Richard. (1988) *The Wake of Imagination.* Minneapolis: University of Minnesota Press. p. 3.
23. Lonergan, Bernard. (1988) *Collection (CW 4)*. p. 241.
24. Lonergan, Bernard. *Insight*. p. 689.

Chapter 4. Creativity and Consciousness – making of our living a work of art

1. An earlier version of this essay was published in *Studies: An Irish Quarterly Review.* Vol. 90 No. 358 Summer 2001. p. 188-196.
2. Carr, Emily. (1946) *Growing Pains.* Toronto: Clarke Irwin & Co., p. 232.
3. Erikson, Erik. (1958) *Young Man Luther.* London: Faber and Faber, p.46.
4. Lonergan, Bernard. (1988) *Collection. (CW 4)*. Toronto: University of Toronto Press, p. 227.
5. Joyce, James. (1916) *A Portrait of the Artist as a Young Man.* edited by Chester B. Anderson (1968) New York: Penguin, Viking Critical Library, p. 247.
6. Ibid., p. 252-253.
7. I am taking the position here that while Stephen Dedalus provided Joyce with a persona for coming to understand his own life experience, he fictionalized much of that experience to suit his own purpose in writing the novel.
8. Lonergan, Bernard. (1993) *Topics in Education (CW 10)*. Edited by Robert M. Doran and Frederick E. Crowe. Toronto: University of Toronto Press. p. 232.
9. McCarthy, Michael. (1990) *The Crisis of Philosophy*. New York: State University of New York Press. p. 227-290. McCarthy accepts Lonergan's *Insight* proposal as a philosophical strategy that will meet the needs of our time. He says that the needs of modernity are met by Lonergan's cognitional theory in that the knower participates in the act of knowing with the hope that reality, truth, *can* be known in a normative unfolding pattern. It is the appropriation of one's own cognitive process that provides a base from which critical meaning can be organized and unified.
10. Lonergan's description of the human mind spiraling through the levels of consciousness by being attentive/intelligent/reasonable provides a heuristic structure of learning. *Heurism* is the word used by philosophers to describe the educational practice of providing tools for students to discover things for themselves. When they have experienced and claimed the workings of their own mind, students have acquired a heuristic structure (a tool) for learning for themselves.

11. Since my concern in here is to explore how levels of consciousness unfold from experience through understanding toward judgment and knowledge, I have chosen to limit the initial discussion of Lonergan's cognitional theory to the first three levels, leaving moral consciousness for later. It seems to make sense pedagogically to give students time to experience/understand/ and come to know the workings of their own minds before tackling the fourth level of moral consciousness of deliberation, evaluation and responsible decision.

12. Lonergan, Bernard. (1985) *A Third Collection: Papers by Bernard J.F. Lonergan, S.J.* edited by Frederick E. Crowe, S.J. New York: Paulist Press. p. 103.

13. Ibid., p. 29.

14. Lonergan, Bernard. (1985) *A Third Collection*. p. 30.

15. The first chapter of *Method* provides Lonergan's latest explanation of the levels of conscious-ness. After twenty five years trying to understand what the terms mean, I think I get it! But I am not sure that I could articulate it to students with any confidence if I had not had the previous experience of repeatedly grinding through *Insight*, especially chapters 1,2,6,7,8,9,11, and reading at least three times *Verbum: Word and Idea in Aquinas. CW 2* (1997).

16. Lonergan, Bernard. (1992) *Insight: A Study of Human Understanding (CW3)* edited by Frederick E. Crowe and Robert M. Doran. Toronto: University of Toronto Press. p. 13.

17. Lonergan, Bernard. (1972) *Method*. p. 265.

18. Lonergan, Bernard. (1990) *Understanding and Being. (CW5)* Edited by Elizabeth A. Morelli and Mark D. Morelli. Toronto: University of Toronto Press. p. 113.

19. Ibid., p. 111.

20. Lonergan, Bernard. (1997) quoting Thomas Aquinas in *Verbum: Word and Idea in Aquinas. (CW2)* Toronto: University of Toronto Press. p. 85.

21. Taylor, Charles. (1989) *Sources of the Self: The Making of the Modern Identity.* Cambridge, MA: Harvard University Press. p. 368-90, 481.

22. Lonergan, Bernard. (1988) *Collection. (CW4)* Edited by Frederick E. Crowe and Robert Doran. Toronto: University of Toronto Press. p. 220.

23. Dunne, Tad. (1998) *What Do I Do When I Paint?* Method: Journal of Lonergan Studies. Vol. 16. p. 103-123. In this article and elsewhere, Tad Dunne has helped me understand Lonergan's thought.

24. Lonergan, Bernard. (1993) *Topics in Education (CW10)* p. 217.

Chapter 5. *Creativity and Values – making of our living a work of art*

1. Heaney, Seamus. (1995) *Crediting Poetry – the Nobel Lecture.* New York: Farrar Straus Giroux, p. 24-26.

2. Lonergan, Bernard. (1972) *Method in Theology.* Toronto: University of Toronto Press. p. 27 and *Topics (CW 10)* p. 33. The choice of the words desire, expectation, value is a pedagogical tool to introduce students to the meaning of the structural components of the human good that Lonergan names particular/order/value.

3. Lonergan, Bernard. *Method*. p. 47-52.

4. Ibid., p. 24.

5. *Method in Theology*, p. 50.

6. One of the Documents of Vatican II (1966) *The Church Today #16* makes the same point. *Conscience is the most secret core and sanctuary of a man (sic). There he is alone with God, whose voice echoes in his depths. ...*

7. Lonergan, Bernard. *Method*. p. 30-34.

8. Lonergan, Bernard. S.J. (1974) *A Second Collection.* Edited by William F.J. Ryan, S.J. and Bernard J. Tyrrell, S.J. Philadelphia: Westminster Press. p. 227.

9. The story of Huck Finn's crisis of conscience is cited by Walter Conn, 'The Desire for Authenticity' in *Desires of the Human Heart.* Edited by Vernon Gregson (1988) New York: Paulist Press p. 36-55.

10. *Method in Theology.* p. 37-38. Lonergan's position on moral consciousness or conscience differs radically from that of Kant and Kohlberg. They understand morality to be the acquisition of rationally (logically) achieved universal principles or maxims such as justice that can be applied in every like-situation. By recognizing the interiority involved in consciousness becoming authentic conscience and by stressing the human capacity for responsible judgments of value, Lonergan takes a different position. As I understand it, when he claims that the good is always concrete, and that humans are free to choose the good, Lonergan allows for the complexity of practical, emotional, imaginative facts that contribute to moral dispositions, judgments and choices. What worries me about current educational practice is the undercurrent of Kohlberg's (derived from Kant's) moral reasoning that has become the basis for the mistaken assumption that values can be taught from outside, without taking into consideration the inner responsibility of the person to gather all the evidence and make one's own judgment.

11. Lonergan, Bernard. *Method.* p. 51.

12. Crowe, Frederick S.J. (1987) Lonergan Workshop Vol. 7. *An Expansion of Lonergan's Notion of Values.* p. 42.

13. Conn, Walter E. (1982) *Conscience: Development and Self-Transcendence.* Birmingham, AL: Religious Education Press. And Robert Kegan. (1982) *The Evolving Self.* Cambridge, MA. Harvard University Press.

14. Lonergan, Bernard. *Faith and Beliefs* mimeographed paper at the Annual Meeting of the American Academy of Religion, Newton, MA. October, 1969. Cited by Walter E. Conn. *Moral Conversion: Development Toward Critical Self-Possession.* Thought. Vol 58 No. 229, June, 1983.

15. Lonergan, Bernard. (1974) *A Second Collection.* p. 83.

16. Ibid., p. 74-75.

17. Arendt, Hannah. (1964) *Eichmann in Jerusalem.* New York: Viking Press, p.126.

18. While I agree with Arendt's critics that using the word "banality" to describe the evil Eichmann accomplished could be interpreted as a trivialization of the phenomenon of the holocaust, her comments in the postscript of the revised edition of her book help me to understand what she meant. I also think that Eichmann as a symbol can help us understand what Lonergan means when he claims that the source of human evil is the contraction of human consciousness and a failure to grasp reality. Arendt writes: *Except for an extraordinary diligence in looking out for his personal advancement, he had no motives at all, he merely never realized what he was doing...he was not stupid...If one cannot extract any diabolical or demonic profundity (hence her use of "banal" to describe what he did) ...that is still far from calling it commonplace...That such remoteness from reality and such thoughtlessness can wreak more havoc than all the evil instincts...which perhaps, are inherent in man – that was in fact the lesson one could learn in Jerusalem.* Ibid., p. 288.

19. Lonergan, Bernard. *Method.* p. 30-34.

20. Lonergan, Bernard. (1974) *A Second Collection.* p. 83.

21. Nova. *The Best Mind Since Einstein,* 1993. WGBM Educational Foundation. Boston.

22. Lonergan, Bernard. (1992) *Insight. (CW 3)* p. 622.

23. Richard Alleva's review of this film gave me this insight into Lavin's character. *"Commonweal"* July 15, 1994.

24. Lonergan, Bernard. (1992) *Insight. (CW 3)* p. 689.

25. Lonergan, Bernard. (1992) *Insight. (CW 3)* p. 570.
26. Lonergan, Bernard. (1992) *Insight. (CW 3)* p. 689.
27. Lonergan, Bernard. (1992) *Insight. (CW 3)* p. 744 *In the twenty-seventh place...besides the image that is a sign of intelligible and rational contents and the image that is a psychic force, there is the image that symbolizes man's orientation into the known unknown...* For Lonergan (and all who accept the Christian belief in the Law of the Cross) the symbol of this orientation is the Crucifix. As I understand it, the death of Jesus "signs" God's love as the higher viewpoint that emerges as a psychic force (grace) empowering believers to accept the reality of evil in the world (the concrete reality of Jesus' death) with hope that it will be an occasion of God's transforming goodness – his resurrection.

Chapter 6. Creativity and Self-Transcendence – where do we go from here?

1. Lonergan, Bernard. (1972) *Method in Theology.* Seabury Press. p. 102.
2. *Method.* p. 106.
3. *Method.* p. 103.
4. *Method.* p. 111.
5. Lonergan, Bernard. (1985) *A Third Collection.* New York: Paulist Press p. 33.
6. *Method.* p. 113.
7. Mathews, William, S.J. *A Biographical Perspective on Conversion and the Functional Specialties in Lonergan.* Method: Journal of Lonergan Studies. Vol. 16, No. 2, Fall 1998. p. 145. I am indebted to William Mathews for his detailed study of this period of Lonergan's life. And of course I heartily support his suggestion that the women who cared for him during this illness made a significant contribution not only to Lonergan's recovery but also to his belief that he was lovable and worthy of care by them and presumably by God.
8. Lonergan, Bernard (1988). *Collection: CW 4.* Edited by Frederick Crowe and Robert Doran. Toronto: University of Toronto Press. p. 223.
9. *Method.* p. 117.
10. Lonergan, Bernard. (1985) *A Third Collection.* p. 55.
11. *Method.* p. 103.

Conclusion

1. Lonergan, Bernard. (1996) *Philosophical and Theological Papers 1958-1964. (CW 6)* edited by Robert Croken, Frederick Crowe and Robert Doran. Toronto: University of Toronto Press. p. 106.
2. Lonergan, Bernard. (1990) *Understanding and Being (CW 5).* Edited by Elizabeth A. Morelli and Mark D. Morelli. Toronto: University of Toronto Press, p. 14.
3. Crowe, Frederick. (1992) *Lonergan.* Collegeville MN: Liturgical Press, p. 74.
4. Lonergan, Bernard. (1993) *Topics in Education (CW 10)* Edited by Robert Doran and Frederick Crowe. Toronto: University of Toronto Press. p. 225.